THE WORLD'S GREATEST
UFO ENCOUNTERS

Photograph Acknowledgements

Fortean Picture Library 8, 9, 54, 55, 59, 60, 62, 69, 72, 92, 93,
97, 102, 104 ttop, 104 bottom, 109 top, 109 bottom,
110 bottom, 111 top, 111 bottom, 112 top, 112 centre,
112 bottom, 122, 127 bottom, 145, 149/Janet & Colin Bord
127 top/Michael Buhler 20/Werner Burger 119/Rod Dickinson
134/Stephen C. Pratt 108/William M. Rebsamen 138/August C.
Roberts 94, 110 top/Dezs Sternoczky 117

THE WORLD'S GREATEST
UFO ENCOUNTERS

Nigel Cawthorne

CHANCELLOR
PRESS

This edition published by Chancellor Press,
an imprint of Bounty Books, a division of
Octopus Publishing Group Ltd,
2-4 Heron Quays, London, E14 4JP

© Octopus Publishing Group Ltd

Printed in 2002 (twice)

ISBN 0 7537 0566 4

Printed and bound in Great Britain by
Mackays of Chatham

Contents

1 Dangerous Liaisons

Protect Yourself

There should be a warning on the side of every UFO that reads: alien encounters can harm your health. And this is not simple paranoia. There are plenty of reports of people being harmed by extra-terrestrials. Sometimes they suffer through exposure to the energy fields associated with UFOs. Then there are the more life-threatening episodes that occur during alien abductions – intrusive examinations, unwanted surgery and the embedding of 'implants' in the body. And sometimes there is outright hostile intent.

Even an innocent UFO sighting can result in psychological problems, including anxiety, mania, depression and post-traumatic stress disorder. In other cases, severe physical effects – burns, eye-sight damage, radiation sickness and even cancer – have been reported. One consistent feature of reports of UFO sightings and alien encounters from across the globe is that they cast the human witness as a victim. Usually, there is little doubt that those involved in such episodes have experienced ill effects; the medical evidence is there for all to see.

Alien Aggression

The first hostile alien encounter took place two months after Kenneth Arnold had first reported seeing flying saucers over the Cascades. In August 1947, geologist Rapuzzi Johannis was climbing the Italian Alps above the village of Villa Santina when he saw a group of aliens. Johannes raised his geologist's pick in greeting,

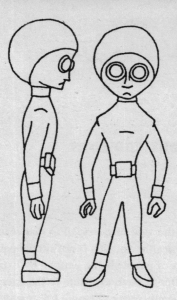

Drawings of two entities seen by Rapuzzi Johannis, August 1947, at Raveo near Villa Santina, Italy.

but his gesture misinterpreted. The aliens immediately fired a beam of light at him that knocked him down the mountainside. Fortunately, his fall was halted by some loose rubble. But the fall left him semi-paralysed and he faced a painful crawl home.

Another unprovoked attack occurred in France on 1 July 1965, when farmer Maurice Masse encountered a similar group of aliens near Valensole. The aliens pointed a 'stick' at him. Although he did not see what happened next, he found himself being flung to the ground. His muscles were paralysed, but he remained conscious.

Too Close for Comfort

On 20 May 1967, a UFO encounter left fifty-two-year-old Canadian engineer Stephen Michalak injured. Michalak's hobby was geology and he was out hunting for minerals near Falcon Lake, eighty miles east of Winnipeg. He heard the sound of geese cackling and looked upwards. He saw two disc-shaped craft hovering overhead. One flew away, but the other landed not far away. Michalak noticed that the object was changing colour as if cooling. He felt waves of heat coming off it. They carried with them a vile, sulphurous odour.

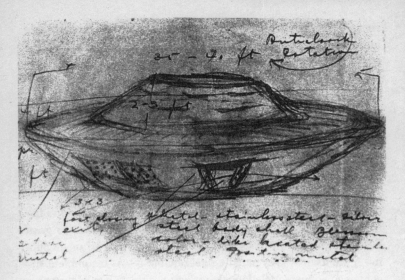

Steve Michalak's sketch of the UFO he saw close-up when it landed near Falcon Lake, Manitoba, Canada, on 20 May 1967.

As Michalak approached the craft, a doorway opened in its side and a brilliant violet light spilled out. The doorway closed again as he got closer. In a foolhardy move, Michalak reached out his hand to touch the surface of the ship. It was hot and he immediately drew his hand back, but his glove had already melted. At that moment, the disc tilted and a blast of light from an 'exhaust panel' in the side hit Michalak in the chest, setting fire to his shirt. He tore off his burning shirt as the spaceship disappeared out of sight.

The two-mile trek back to the highway was agonising and Michalak vomited countless times. When he returned to Winnipeg he was treated for first-degree burns and released. Two days later he returned to the doctor suffering from a mysterious malady. The doctor prescribed pain-killers and sea-sickness tablets, which were of little help. For several days after the incident he was unable to keep his food down and he lost twenty-two pounds in weight. His blood lymphocyte count was down from twenty-five per cent to sixteen per cent. Medical reports also showed that he had skin infections and rashes. He suffered from nausea, diarrhoea, generalised urticaria and blackouts, and generally felt weak and dizzy. He also experienced numbness and chronic swelling of the joints. Then, in August 1968 – fifteen months after the encounter – a geometric pattern of burns appeared on his chest.

Over eighteen months, Michalak was examined by a total of twenty-seven doctors, at a cost of thousands of dollars, but none explained the cause of his symptoms. The case was also investigated by a number of government departments.

The Canadian Department of National Defense examined the encounter site. They found higher than normal background radiation, along with silver fragments that had been exposed to great heat. The full results of their investigations were never made public. A file itself was eventually released, but it was incomplete and contained so many deletions that it was not much use. However, a number of independent researchers have pointed out that Michalak's symptoms are reminiscent of radiation exposure. If this was the case, Michalak is far from alone in experiencing these symptoms after an encounter with a UFO.

Blinded by the Light

On the evening of 7 January 1970, two unfortunate skiers were out on the wooded slopes near the village of Imjarvi, Finland. The temperature was far below freezing that night and Esko Viljo and Aarno Heinonen had stopped briefly at the base of a slope to try and warm themselves when, suddenly, the air was filled with a strange buzzing sound. Then they saw a glowing light surrounded by mist, spiralling downwards into a clearing. The fog began to spread out through the woods and the sound increased in pitch. Then, through the mist, a strange figure appeared. The encounter was cut short by a silent but dazzling explosion of light. It blasted the mist apart, leaving Viljo and Heinonen shrouded in darkness.

The shock was too much for Heinonen, who had been closer to the explosion. He stumbled forward and collapsed. One side of his body was completely paralysed. Viljo helped him to his feet and, together, they began to trudge back to the village.

It was an arduous journey in their enfeebled state. On the way, Heinonen's condition worsened, and the two men were forced to abandon their skis. By the time they reached the village, Heinonen was seriously ill. He was vomiting frequently. His head was pounding and he found that his urine was discoloured. One doctor who examined Heinonen noted that he exhibited the symptoms of radiation sickness, but could find no obvious cause, and, eventually, the symptoms disappeared.

Although Viljo had been further away, he had not escaped unscathed. There were problems with his eyes and he suffered excessive tiredness. The both men suffered post-traumatic stress, which badly affected their memories. But gradually, some recollection of the small, wax-coloured alien they had seen inside the glowing mist came back to them. This, they were sure, was the cause of the medical problems.

One theory was that they had encountered some entirely natural phenomenon that, as well as causing their physical injuries, had triggered a vivid hallucination. Professor Stig Lundquist of the University of Uppsala in Sweden considered that option in the Heinonen and Viljo case. The incident occurred up in the region of the Northern Lights and he investigated local atmospheric conditions, but he concluded that these were unlikely to be the cause of the incident:

'I do not think that I can explain the phenomenon as being naturally occurring,' he said.

Cornish Contretemps

On 17 September 1977, Caroline Bond and Peter Boulter suffered a similar encounter. The young couple were doing some work on an old post-office in the village of Newmill in Cornwall. Caroline was astride her moped, about to ride off, when she felt her skin tingle. She looked around to see a strange green mist drifting towards her, a few inches off the ground.

She leapt off her moped and ran back inside the building, screaming that she had just seen a ghost. Peter could hardly take this seriously, but he could see her terror was very real. When he went outside to take look, he saw a strange light soaring away into the sky. It was travelling relatively slowly and took a long time to disappear. So he went back inside and watched it from an upstairs window. It was then he noted that the light was no longer alone. It now seemed to have smaller red lights alongside it.

Meanwhile, Caroline, who had recovered her composure, leapt back on her moped and set off in pursuit. On the way, she came across several other villagers who had also seen the strange light, though none of them had had her ringside seat.

Soon after the encounter, Peter and Caroline became seriously ill. They suffering aching muscles, pounding headaches, vomiting and other symptoms that had been reported in the Finnish case. Peter went though a series of exhaustive tests, but nothing could be found. Eventually the mystery illness cleared up without treatment. Caroline, who had been closer, was more seriously affected. The possibility of appendicitis was considered. She was operated on and her appendix removed although, on examination, it seemed perfectly healthy. After some weeks, she began to recover. Nevertheless, the trauma of the encounter remained with the two of them for many years even though they had not seen any aliens or even anything that they could identify as a spacecraft.

Attack in the Forest

Scottish forester Bob Taylor was another victim. While working in the woodlands outside Livingston in West Lothian on 9 November 1979, Taylor came upon a strange egg-shaped object about twenty feet across in a clearing. It 'faded in and out of reality', he said, as he watched. Then two dark objects around a foot in diameter with six legs, like old-fashioned sea mines, sped towards him. They were round with spikes. He was knocked to the ground and remembered feeling a strange pulling sensation on his legs. When he came to, Taylor was alone, but he found himself in a terrible state. His trousers were torn. His head was pounding and his legs felt like jelly. Partially paralysed, he had to drag himself home painfully along the ground.

The police were called in. A major inquiry followed and the site of the encounter was cordoned off like a crime scene while the forensic team went over it. They found mysterious triangular indentations in the ground. Taylor's trousers were sent away for forensic analysis. However, the police eventually reported that they could find no evidence of an alien force, even though the credibility of the witness and the physical effects that he suffered were undoubted. Like the previous victims, he eventually recovered.

Burning Ring of Fire

On 13 March 1980, a sub-contractor was driving home from Worcester to Stratford-upon-Avon. When he passed near the village of Haselor, he had a close encounter. A cigar-shaped white craft surrounded by a red glow flashed passed his car. It was so big it filled the windscreen. As it passed by, the steering wheel suddenly became unbearably hot – a burning ring of fire. He let go and the car swerved. His hands suffered serious burns.

Scientists have explained that fluctuating magnetic fields produced by the UFO induced electrical eddy currents inside the metal steering wheel, heating it up. Such an intense field could have caused all sorts of other health problems if the UFO had hung around longer.

The ABC of After-Effects

The after-effects of alien abductions can have serious long-term effects. American UFOlogist Jerome Clark divides them into three stages. The initial stage, which Clark calls 'immediate after-effects', usually involves physical problems, such as nausea, irritated eyes, an unusual thirst, scoop-like cuts in the legs and nose-bleeds that can last days or weeks.

The second stage, 'intermediate after-effects', usually start a few weeks or even months after the abduction. It is then that the psychological difficulties begin. These include recurring nightmares, flashbacks, panic attacks and an irrational anxiety when returning to the area of the abduction – even though the victim may have no conscious memory of the event itself. Even so, this stage is often marked by the obsessive need to return to the site of the abduction, as if the victim is willing it to happen again.

The final stage in Clark's outline are the 'long-term effects'. These can occur years after the abduction and often involve changes in the personality and outlook of the abductee. Often these changes can be for the better. Some abductees have discovered hidden artistic talents or a previously unacknowledged spiritual side to their nature.

Stage One and Two

UFOlogist Leonard Stringfield encountered stage-one after-effects after Mona Stafford, Elaine Thomas and Louise Smith had been abducted by a UFO while driving down Route 78 in Kentucky on 6 January 1976. They wanted to keep their story a secret but information was leaked to the local press. Stringfield picked up on the story and persuaded them to meet him on 29 February.

'The effects of the close encounter were still painfully apparent,' said Stringfield. 'They looked drained and tense.' All three women had experienced severe weight loss, and Smith had what Stringfield described as 'a round, pinkish-grey blotch' on her body.

Smith also suffered second-stage effects, which lured her back to the site of the encounter, where she seems to have been abducted again. On 28 January she was in bed asleep when she was woken by strange voices. They urged her to get dressed and drive back to Route 78. Once she arrived at the site of the encounter, she stood there not knowing what to do. A feeling of terror came over her and she felt a pulling at her hands. Then she fled back to her car and drove off. She later noticed that three rings were missing from her hand – rings that normally required lubricating with soap before they could be removed.

Stafford, too, suffered second-stage effects. Disturbing mental images came and went. For a while she moved back in with her parents but, when she returned to her trailer, she was woken one night by 'mental voices'. A bright light came flooding in through the doorway and she saw a small being standing there.

Epilepsy

MUFON's Robert J. Durrant has suggested that encounters or abductions may cause temporal lobe epilepsy. Unlike normal epileptic attacks, when the victim suffers fits, convulsions and unconsciousness, TLE often produces hallucinatory effects. This is because the temporal lobe is not connected to any muscles that can convulse. Instead, it controls higher functions of the brain, such as memory and learning. Durrant has studied Whitley Strieber's auto-biographical accounts of his abduction experiences, *Transformation* and *Majestic*, and says that all the symptoms of temporal lobe epilepsy are present in Strieber's writings. These include floating sensations, paranormal experiences, anomalous smells, enhanced imagination and episodes that seem to have intense personal meaning. However, Strieber has undergone two series of tests for TLE. Both of them proved negative. This has led to the suggestion that aliens communicate telepathically with their abductees through the temporal lobe, hence the similarities between TLE and abduction experiences.

Implants

One of the most obvious after-effects of abductions is the discovery of an alien object implanted in the body of the abductee. Chief of Abduction Investigations for the Houston UFO Network, Derrel Sims has spent twenty-five years investigating abductions, and has himself been abducted. Implants are his field. In 1995 he called in Dr Roger Leir to remove two objects from an abductee known as Mrs Connely. Although her abduction had occurred twenty-five years before, in 1970, until the implants showed up on an X-ray, she had no idea of their existence. The T-shaped objects were found in her toe. They were about a fifth of an inch in height and made from an ultra-hard, unidentifiable metal, which was highly magnetic. The implants were sheathed in a dense, dark grey membrane that could not be cut with a sharp scalpel. Mysteriously, they were attached to nerve endings in a part of the body where no nerves are known to exist. Mrs Connely's case might help to explain why scoop-like scars are frequently found on the lower leg area ofabductees.

Unexplained Pregnancies

Perhaps the most disturbing of the after-effects of alien abductions are unexplained pregnancies. The evidence indicates that our extra-terrestrial intruders are running a programme to create a human–alien hybrid. There are numerous reports of aliens abducting women, impregnating them, returning them home, then abducting them again a few months later to take the foetus. This has a devastating affect on the women involved.

One such is Indiana housewife Kathie Davis. One evening in 1977, at around 9:30 p.m., she saw a light about the size of a base-ball floating around her backyard. She went outside to look for it. She spent no more than ten minutes looking for it then, finding nothing, went to a friend's house for a moonlight swim. But when she arrived it was already 11 p.m. More than hour of her life was missing. Later, when she returned home from the swim, she felt an inexplicable chill and a fogging of the vision. Later she recalled an abduction experience. Neighbours confirmed this. They had seen a flash of light and felt their house vibrate as if there had been an earth tremor.

Kathie recalled being given a gynaecological examination by aliens. Abduction expert Budd Hopkins believes that she was impregnated by the aliens. A few months, she was abducted again. This time, during a second examination, she reported feeling a ter-rible pressure inside her. Then, under hypnosis, she became dis-turbed and cried out: 'It's not fair. It's mine.'

Later, she began having disturbing dreams. In them, she gave birth to a weird-looking, super-intelligent hybrid. Other abductees also reported dreaming of giving birth to so-called wise babies. Later Kathie recalled having a phantom pregnancy when she was teenager. When she was abducted years later she was intro-duced to a half-alien half-human hybrid that she recognised was her daughter.

In November 1983 she was abducted once again. This time the aliens removed some of her ova. During an abduction in April 1986, she was shown two elf-like infants. She was told that these were her children, too. The aliens told her they had nine of her offspring altogether. Although none of Kathie's extraterrestrial pregnancies was confirmed medically, she was left with a series of unexplainable scars that had resulted from the experience.

Lethal Encounter

At around 11:30 p.m. on 17 March 1978, service engineer Ken Edwards left the M62 motorway at the turn off to Risley. He was on his way home from a trade union meeting in Cheshire. His route took him through a deserted industrial area, much of which was derelict. As he passed the vast Atomic Energy Authority complex, his headlights picked out a weird figure, standing alone at the top of an embankment. Edwards stopped his van to investigate.

The creature was over seven feet tall and did not look human. Its arms came out of the top of its shoulders. Its body was silver, but its head was black and shaped like a goldfish bowl. It held its arms out ahead like a sleepwalker, then start walking down the embankment. The odd thing was that it walked at right angles to the steep slope, but did not topple forward.

When it reached the road, Edwards noticed that it had no knee joints. Its legs articulated from the hips, making its movement rather stiff. Then the creature stopped. It turned its head towards Edwards. Two pencil-thin beams of light shot out its eye socket. The beams came straight through the windscreen and hit Edwards full on. The effect was immediate.

'My head was swimming with strange thoughts,' he said. 'There were hundreds of them, all racing through my mind at once. I also felt very odd. It was a sensation like two enormous hands pressing down on me from above. The pressure was tremendous. It seemed to paralyse me. I could only move my eyes. The rest of me was rigid.'

The creature then carried on across the road. It walked straight through a ten-foot-high security fence as if it was not there, and vanished into the trees beyond. At this point, Edwards' mind went blank.

The next thing he recalled was arriving home at around half-past midnight. He had no idea how he had got there. He walked into the house, where his wife Barbara was waiting for him. She was anxious and could have been angry, but she noticed the state he was in. When he saw his wife, he blurted out: 'I've seen a silver man.' This sounded crazy and his 'missing time' story sounded a bit thin. But when they noticed that his watch had stopped at exactly 11:45 p.m., she took it seriously.

The couple went to the local police station. The duty officer thought the story was crazy too, but Edwards' obvious sincerity impressed him. The police contacted the atomic plant and Edwards reluctantly agreed to go back to the scene of the encounter with them. They were met by a team of twenty-five AEA security guards who carried batons. When Edwards related his incredible story, not one of them so much as smirked. Then they made a cursory search of the area, but they refused to go into the trees where Edwards had seen the creature disappear.

It turned out that the AEA complex was a UFO hotspot. Eight sightings had been reported in the area around that time. And four local youths had seen a cigar-shaped craft flying over the plant on the day of Edwards' encounter. Two police constables, Rob Thompson and Roy Kirckpatrick, followed up several leads. They checked out nearby Warrington College in case the students there had pulled some stunt, but they were not holding a rag week at the time and no link was established. Edwards was not impressed by this line of investigation.

'I wish they could tell me how they did it,' he said. 'How they blew up my radio and walked through a fence, some stunt.'

The police also wondered whether Edwards had seen a fireman clad in a silver radiation suit. They took him to the AEA complex and, without warning, had a member of staff in a silver fireman's suit walk out in front of the car. Edwards was unfazed.

'It was nothing like it,' he said.

Unable to shed any further light the matter, the police closed the case.

But the case was far from closed for Edwards. The 'missing' forty-five minutes between his watch stopping and the time he arrived home troubled him. He worried that he might have been abducted. But he could not simply put the matter out of his mind. He had physical proof that something had happened. The beams from the creature's eyes had damaged both him and his vehicle.

Where he had gripped the steering wheel, Edwards's fingers were bright red, as if badly sunburned. After the encounter he found that the van's two-way radio did not work. When an electrician examined it, he discovered that the circuit board was burned out. The probable cause of this, he speculated, was an enormous power surge through the aerial.

Then, less than a year after his strange encounter, Edwards fell ill. He lost all energy and began to suffer from stomach cramps. When he went to hospital, the doctors diagnosed cancer of the kidneys. In 1980, Edwards underwent major surgery. All seemed well but, after a couple of months, cancer cells appeared in his throat. The disease seemed unstoppable. Four years after the encounter with the silver-suited alien, Edwards was dead.

UFO investigators Peter Hough and Jenny Randles later discovered that unusual experiments were being carried out in a building near the AEA complex. But no one will say whether an experiment was underway that night.

Death Ray

The Edwards' case is reminiscent of another encounter when a victim was zapped in Brazil. On 13 August 1967, forty-one-year-old Ignacio de Souza and his young wife Louisa were returning to their ranch at Pilar de Goias, Brazil. The ranch had its own landing strip, but the couple were astounded to see that what had landed on it in their absence was no ordinary aircraft. What they saw was a spacecraft that looked like 'an upturned wash basin' on the runway. Near to it, were three alien entities wearing yellow ski suits.

De Souza loosed off a shot at one of them with the .44 carbine he was carrying. The UFO fired back and he was hit by a green beam that came from the craft. Realising that their reception was far from friendly, the aliens then climbed into the spaceship and it took off. Until the encounter de Souza had been good health. But afterwards, he suffered from nausea and uncontrollable shaking.

He was flown to hospital in nearby Goiana for tests. He had leukaemia and died two months later.

Grievous Bodily Harm

Probably the best-known UFO encounter that caused harm to humans involved restaurant owner Betty Cash, her friend Vickie Landrum and her grandson, Colby. The case received enormous media coverage worldwide because the victims sued the US government for $20 million.

The deadly encounter took place on the chilly night of 29 December 1980, when Betty, Vickie and Colby were driving down an isolated section of Highway 1485, which took them though a pine and oak forest near Huffman, Texas, some fifteen miles outside Houston. The two middle-aged women and the young boy had had their evening meal at a roadside restaurant in nearby New Caney and were now heading towards home in Dayton. At around 9 p.m., they had just rounded a bend in the highway,

Interpretation of UFO event by artist Michael Buhler: Huffman, Texas.

when ten-year-old Colby pointed out a blazing light in the sky. A huge diamond-shaped vessel loomed in front of them. It descended to tree-top level, straddling the road. They found their way blocked by a jet of fire that looked like the exhaust of a space rocket.

Cash, who was driving, stopped the car less than sixty yards from the mysterious object, which glowed so brightly that, in the surrounding forest, it could have been day. The three of them got out of the car to investigate, only to be met by a wave of tremendous heat. Colby became distressed and Vickie Landrum got back into the car with him. But Betty Cash continued to gaze mesmerised at the dazzling object, even though the intense heat was burning her skin and the bright light was damaging her eyes. It was only when the object began to move that Cash heard Landrum's pleas and returned to the car. But as Cash touched the handle of the car door, she found it was red hot and burned her hand. Her wedding ring also burned into her finger.

The craft then made a loud roaring noise. As it took off into night sky, some two dozen unmarked black helicopters swept into view. The three witnesses later identified them as CH-47 Chinook twin-blades, and they were either pursuing or escorting the mysterious craft. Cash set off in pursuit of the unidentified aircraft and the fleet of dark helicopters. After a mile or so they had to turn onto a larger highway. One of the helicopters turned back and buzzed the car, deafening the passengers with the roar of its engines. They got the message, turned off the highway and headed home.

All three of them were stunned and bewildered by the encounter. At first they thought it must have been a hallucination, but then they learned that, in the outskirts of Houston, residents had also seen bright lights and helicopters in the sky that night. Then there were the injuries that they had sustained from the strange encounter.

Cash's eyes were so swollen that she unable to see for a week. She suffered from vomiting and diarrhoea, various aches and pains, blistering of the scalp and temporary hair loss. Three days after the encounter, her condition deteriorated to the point that she checked into the emergency room of a nearby hospital. Betty did not tell the-hospital doctors about her UFO encounter – they treated her as a classic burns victim, until Colby revealed what had happened. Vickie Landrum and Colby also exhibited burns, although to a lesser extent. Both had swollen eyes and suffered vomiting and diarrhoea, and Vickie had some hair loss. When the three of them were examined, it was discovered that their symptoms were consistent with exposure to ultra-violet, microwave and X-ray radiation. Later Betty suffered cataracts and developed breast cancer and had to have a mastectomy.

A few months later, Cash and Landrum sued the US government for $20 million in medical compensation for the injuries they had suffered, with the help of Peter Gersten, a lawyer who specialises in UFO cases. The lawsuit proved to be a long and drawn-out one. Although it was ultimately a futile exercise, officers from every branch of the services were dragged into court. They insisted that the US military was neither involved in or responsible for what had happened. Finally, in 1986, a judge dismissed the case on the grounds that Cash and Landrum could not prove the 'UFO' that had caused them injury was the property of the US government. However, this ignored the presence of the Chinooks.

While the US government is in full-scale denial of the facts, the UFO community has broken into four factions when it comes to the Cash–Landrum case. One faction believes that they saw a top-secret nuclear-powered US military aircraft with extraterrestrial connections. Another faction believes that they witnessed the test-flight of a US military spacecraft back-engineered by US scientists from their examination of alien wreckage. An anonymous US intelligence office apparently confessed: 'The craft was an alien craft piloted by military aircraft pilots.'

A third faction believes that what they saw was a UFO intruder being shepherded out of US airspace by the military, while a fourth say what the Texas trio saw was one of the many manoeuvres conducted by the ultra-top-secret alliance between the US government and an alien force. All four agree that the helicopters were there to seal off the area in the event that the mysterious craft was somehow forced to land.

Houston-based Boeing aerospace engineer John Schuessler, a thirty-five-year veteran of many UFO investigations, studied the case and concluded that what Cash and Landrum had seen was a UFO, which may or may not have been in difficulty. The US military had deployed a fleet of helicopters to follow it and Cash, Landrum and Colby suffered injuries as a direct result of their encounter.

He discovered the helicopters came from Fort Hood, in Waco, Texas, and from an aircraft carrier anchored in the Gulf of Mexico – a vessel he cannot name. Schuessler says that the military helicopters were on a monitoring mission. The aliens are now here in such force that, although the US government is in communication with them, it can do nothing to prevent their frequent sorties. Schuessler discounts the idea that the aliens are here to create a new hybrid species using the terrestrial gene pool. Nor does he believe that the aliens are out to destroy us, although they are exploiting our resources in a number of mysterious ways. But the US government can do little more than keep tabs on their foraging expeditions – one of which was witnessed by Cash, Landrum and Colby.

Schuessler interviewed Air Force generals and congressmen, who gave him a lot of answers – but many of them turned out to be contradictory or downright lies. This convinced him that there was something to the story, or why would senior figures go to such great lengths to deny it? He pursued the matter through covert sources, who confirmed the story. But none of them would make any on-the-record admission. Nor could the government admit its impotence in court. However, a helicopter pilot came forward to give details of what had happened that night, but subsequently recanted. 'Obviously, his superiors shut him up,' Schuessler said.

Reviewing the witnesses' injuries, Schuessler said: 'Betty Cash's after-effects were the most drastic because she was out the car for the longest period of time and was exposed directly to the UFO. Within twenty-four hours, she had swelling, blisters on the face and sunburn. She was vomiting for weeks and, after three weeks, a large amount of her hair fell out. In the years that followed, she suffered twenty-five to thirty hospitalisations, many of them in intensive care. She developed cancer and a low red blood cell count, she had bone marrow problems and then, eventually, she had a stroke.'

He believes that her illnesses were cause by exposure to some kind of radiation.

'I am not saying it was ionising radiation,' he said. 'The electromagnetic spectrum has a wide range of radiation that one can be exposed to. At first, the doctors were totally baffled and the initial doctor she went to in emergency care actually consulted other doctors who understood UFOs. Her long-term doctor, who was an expert in the field of radiation sickness, felt that she had been exposed to ionising radiation because her skin had the texture and the feel of it. She couldn't have skin grafts on the burns because of the texture of her skin.'

He could not get any more out of the doctors, for fear of breaching patient confidentiality, but they believed that the injuries were genuine and not self-inflicted.

With no federal money to compensate them, Betty Cash, Vickie Landrum and Colby tried to rebuild their lives. After years of drifting, Cash returned to live with her family in seclusion in Alabama. Throughout this unsettled time, she was dogged by ill-health. She contracted cancer, which she was certain was induced her UFO encounter and also suffered a near-fatal heart attack. She said these illnesses, together with intrusion by the press and assaults by the government on her credibility in the years following her encounter, virtually destroyed her life. She died on 29 December 1998, eighteen years to the day after her UFO encounter.

Vickie Landrum has also suffered health problems since the encounter. Like Cash, she too drifted from place to place for years, before disappearing into a very private life.

Only Colby appears to have come through unscathed. He suffered no long-term ill effects from the encounter and held down a good job in Houston, Texas. However, he refuses to talk about his experience.

'Many people have been injured emotionally as well as physically by their encounters with UFOs and have had their lives devastated,' says Sue Pitts, Alabama assistant state director for the Mutual UFO Network. She tells the story of Falkville police chief Jeff Greenhaw who photographed and chased an alien in 1973.

'Folks thought Jeff was hoaxed or was himself lying,' says Pitts. 'He lost his job. His wife divorced him. For years he's lived in seclusion in Alabama, refusing interviews.'

The sad case of Betty Cash, Vickie Landrum and Colby is far from an isolated one. In the 1994 book *Taken*, author Karla Turner describes symptoms similar to those exhibited by Betty Cash that were suffered by a number of women abductees. Four of them reported waking up with badly irritated eyes. Two of them suffered inexplicable 'sunburn' and sudden hair losses. One, 'Beth', woke up the morning after her abduction with a pounding headache, aching muscles and dizziness. She felt extreme nausea and suffered from diarrhoea and repeated vomiting. He eyes were so badly swollen that she could not see. The parallels to Cash's symptoms are so close that some have suggested that Cash, Landrum and Colby were abducted.

Curiously, another of Turner's abductees, 'Amelia', reported lying in bed surrounded by light – she was not alone and this was witnessed by friends. The ceiling then opened. She looked up to see a helicopter with two aliens inside. She could describe the helicopter and the aliens, but her friends were dazzled by the light and saw nothing more.

Silver Linings

The effects of a UFO encounter, or an alien abduction, are not necessarily harmful. In some cases victims have reported that the experience has changed their life for the better. They have discovered hitherto unknown artistic talents, the development of psychic skills, a new awareness of environmental issues and profound lifestyle changes. Some UFOlogists argue that these beneficial transformations may actually hold the key to a true understanding of UFO phenomena as a whole.

One such transformation was experienced by Peter Holding. As a teenager, he had a number of UFO encounters including an abduction-like experience. In the middle of the night, Holding woke suddenly and experienced an overwhelming compulsion to go to the window. When he opened the curtains, he noticed that there was no glass in the window. In its place was a mesmerising bright light with colours swirling around it. The next thing he knew the image had disappeared and the window had glass in it again. Soon after, Holding developed a previously undetected artistic talent for painting and photography. His works often incorporate the swirling image he saw during the encounter. He found that he could sell his paintings. His photographs have been published and he won a bursary to study art. It became his career, though he had no thought of becoming an artist until after the encounter.

Betty Andreason developed a talent for drawing after her abduction. A similar transformation was experienced by another witness known in the literature only as Bryan. He had had a lifelong history of UFO encounters and, during his adolescence, had a number of night-time visits from extraterrestrial entities. These encounters heralded a sudden explosion of artistic talent. He excelled at art school and went on to make his living by painting.

Psychic Powers

Many abductees have also shown a marked increase in their psychic awareness and abilities after their encounter. Dr John E. Mack, Professor of Psychiatry at Harvard Medical School, has come across several cases in his extensive work with abductees. One of his subjects was a woman named Eva. She had several UFO encounters. After an abduction, she developed telepathic contact with the alien entities. This has opened a gateway to a wide range of paranormal phenomena. She began to see ghosts and, during a near-death experience, she saw a doorway into another dimension.

One famous psychic who now attributes his astonishing powers to a UFO encounter is world-famous spoon-bender Uri Geller. One day when he was four or five years old and was living in Tel Aviv, Israel, he went into the overgrown garden across the road from the apartment block where he lived. He heard kittens crying and walked towards the sound. Then, suddenly, he felt something hovering above him. When he looked up, he saw a ball of light, not the sun, but a pulsating sphere of light in the air. Years later he could still remember this vividly.

'I remember all the sounds stopped, as if time itself had stopped,' he says. 'I looked at this thing for about ten seconds when, suddenly, a beam shot out of it and hit my forehead and knocked me back. It didn't hurt, it just pushed me back on to the ground.'

He suffered no physical after-effects, but soon afterwards, spoons started to bend in his hands. Geller is convinced that his experience was responsible. And he has a number of theories.

'My most bizarre theory is that the energy is coming from a higher intelligence, maybe extraterrestrial in form,' he says. 'Maybe a baby extraterrestrial that ran away from its parents is playing havoc with me and my life.'

Brazilian psychic Thomaz Green Morton, who is one of the world's most gifted paranormal practitioners, also believes that he got his prodigious powers from an extraterrestrial source. He was struck by a beam of light from a strange cloud while out fishing. Since then he has been able to perform psychokinesis and materialisation, and he has been investigated by numerous scientists, including NASA astronaut Dr Brian O'Leary.

Like Uri Geller, he can bend metal objects just by holding them. He can also transform a dollar bill into a bill made up of numerous other world currencies fused together. His favourite trick is to manifest perfume, which pours from his skin. In front of a camera and under the strictest scientific conditions, he can take a regular egg and materialise a chick inside it, which then breaks out of the shell.

Healing Powers

Other abductees have developed mediumship, dowsing abilities and healing powers after their encounters. In one case in 1978 Elsie Oakensen encountered a dumb-bell-shaped UFO while driving on a motorway in Northamptonshire. She was struck by the light of the object as it hovered above her car. Then quite spontaneously it disappeared. At the time, she thought it was just a brief encounter, but later she discovered that it had lasted a couple of hours. Within days, she developed spectacular healing abilities. She even cured her granddaughter, who was deaf, after doctors had suggested that no cure was likely. Oakensen was sure she had no such ability before.

Sometimes a UFO encounter has a more direct beneficial effect. Witnesses have reported miracle cures simply from seeing a UFO. In one striking case, an American law enforcement officer was pursing a UFO, when he was zapped by an energy beam at close quarters. Shortly before, a pet alligator had inflicted a painful bite on his hand. After the encounter, the bite mark was gone. The wound had spontaneous healed. It is thought that the intense energy fields that UFOs generate could be harnessed in the same way that radiotherapy is now used.

Much the same thing happened to a famous French biochemist. He told the story of his miracle cure to French UFOlogist Aimé Michel, who was allowed to publish an account of the abduction, only provided that he did not use his name and identified him as 'Dr X'.

In 1968, Dr X was thirty-eight and was living with his wife and fourteen-month-old son in a house overlooking a valley in southeast France. On the night of 2 November 1968, he awoke to hear the cries of his son. There was a thunderstorm going on outside. His wife was sound asleep, so Dr X got up to attend to the child. He did so with some difficulty. A couple of days before he had been chopping wood and had slipped. The axe had struck his left leg, bursting an artery and causing extensive internal bleeding. The wound had been treated by a doctor, who had examined it again the previous afternoon.

He already had problems with his right leg. During the Algerian war, a mine had exploded, fracturing his skull. This damaged the left hemisphere of his brain, paralysing the right side of his body. The paralysis passed after a couple of months, but left the muscles of his right side permanently wasted. This cost him a career as a musician and he could not stand on his right leg alone. Even so, he managed to totter to his son's room.

The boy was standing up in his crib, shouting, 'Rho, rho'.

This was the word the child used for a fire in the hearth or any bright light. He was pointing to the window. Dr X assumed he was indicating the lightning flashes that were visible through the cracks in the shutters. He got the boy some water and settled him down again. He could hear a shutter blowing back and forth in the breeze. It was in an upstairs room. He went up and closed it, noticing, in his half-asleep state, that the room was bathed in a pulsating light.

After closing the shutter, he felt thirsty and went downstairs to get a drink of water. Still puzzled by the pulsating light, he went out onto the terrace to investigate. It was 3:55 a.m. by the kitchen clock, he noted. Outside, he immediately saw the source of the flashing light. It was being emitted by two disc-shaped silver UFOs that hovered over the valley. They had long antennae sprouting from them. These seemed to be collecting electricity from the storm clouds. A glow would start at the furthest end of the antenna, build up along its length, then discharge suddenly as a lightning bolt to the ground. The build up happened rhythmically and the discharge bathed the whole valley with a pulsating light.

The two craft merged into one and the pulsating ceased. The united object then moved up the valley towards him. Dr X saw the underside was covered with rotating dark bands, causing patterns that defied the laws of science and logic. When the craft got within five hundred yards of Dr X, he began to feel that it had noticed him. It turned a bright beam of light on him, which bathed the whole house in an intense glow. He raised his hands to protect his eyes. Then there was a loud bang and the craft shot skywards so fast that it appeared to be a single streak of light.

When Dr X went back inside it was 4:05 am. He did not think that he had been outside for one minute, let alone ten. He went back upstairs and woke his wife. He told her what he had seen. As he talked excitedly to her, he paced up and down, stopping every so often to make notes and draw sketches of what he had seen. Suddenly, his wife noticed that he was walking normally. He pulled up his pyjama leg. The axe wound had healed completely. This was impossible in such a short time. What is more, his withered right leg was functioning perfectly too.

However, the encounter seemed to have disturbed him psychologically and he experienced some form of amnesia. After Dr X went back to bed, his wife noticed that he was talking in his sleep. She noted down what it was saying. One of the things he repeated was: 'Contact will be re-established by falling downstairs on 2 November.'

She did not tell him about this. When he awoke at 2 p.m. the next day, she suggested that he should write to the UFOlogist Aimé Michel, who was a friend. Why should he do that, he asked. His wife then discovered that he had lost all recollection of the UFO sighting the previous night. When she showed him the notes and sketches he had made, he grew alarmed.

Later that afternoon, Dr X tripped and fell down the stairs. It was as if something had grabbed his leg, he said. He hit his head and suddenly total recall of his experiences the previous night flooded back into his head.

However, there were other worrying effects from a subsequent encounter. Twelve days later, he dreamed about seeing another UFO. It was not like the ones he had seen. It was bright, luminous and triangular. Three days after that, he felt an itching sensation on his stomach. The following day a red triangle appeared around his navel. The dermatologist was baffled and wanted to write a scientific paper about it. Dr X prevented him.

Dr X contacted his friend Aimé Michel, who discovered that there had been a rash of UFO sightings around the area the night Dr X had seen his flying saucers. He suggested that the red triangle might be psychosomatic in origin. Dr X agreed, only to find that a similar red mark had appeared on his son's stomach the next day.

The experience left Dr X depressed and confused. The triangle disappeared, but reappeared every so often. Gradually Dr X began to take an interest in ecology. Other injuries he suffered healed up miraculously. However he has become sensitive to poltergeists and ghosts in the house. Aliens also pay visits and take him on journeys over impossible distances.

Spiritual Fulfilment

Sometimes the after-effects are more subtle, such as an urge to find greater spiritual fulfilment. One of Dr Mack's subjects, named Lee, found that a classical, intrusive abduction spiritually transformed her life. She told Dr Mack that the encounter was 'a priceless opportunity for spiritual growth and sensitivity to all sentient beings, ranging from insects to those of other dimensions and planetary systems'.

Another of Mack's subjects, Catherine, said that her abduction had boosted her intuition and given her a 'greater sensitivity to other people's auras'. In his assessment of the case, Dr Mack said: 'The acceptance of the actuality of her experiences, whatever their source may ultimately prove to be, has permitted Catherine to deal more effectively with the powerful effects and bodily feelings that accompany them and to reach a higher, or more creative, level of consciousness.'

Debbie Jordan had a spiritual awakening of a more religious nature. She had suffered multiple abductions, beginning in childhood, and was once artificially inseminated by an alien. Even so, she has drawn spiritual nourishment from it.

'The experiences changed from being physical in nature to being more mental, psychological, psychic and spiritual,' she said in an interview in 1996. 'I have since become aware of being taught Hinduism and Eastern religions I didn't have any previous knowledge of at all.' Now she has no terror of further abductions. 'It's like going to school. It opens my mind. It's changing everything about me inside – the way I look at life and God and myself and my fellow man.'

Another abductee reported more practical results of this alien education. During her abduction she was interrogated by the aliens. If she answered their questions, the extraterrestrials said, they would answer some of hers.

'We went on like this for quite a while,' she said. 'Because I left school at fourteen, I never learned anything. Anything I did learn, I learned through these experiences. In fact, without these experiences, I would be illiterate. I wouldn't have any interest in maths or history or anything like that.'

Positive lifestyle changes are also reported. Abductees frequently convert to vegetarianism or give up smoking; others change their attitude to the work they do and change career as a result. This happened to Elaine and John Avis after they and their three children were abducted in 1974. Driving on the outskirts of London, the family saw a light in the sky. Their car was then engulfed in a green mist. Again, although they thought this was a momentary experience, they discovered later that it had lasted two hours. Regressional hypnosis revealed an abduction, during which the family members underwent a thorough medical examination at the hands of the alien. But instead of being traumatised, the family members acquired a new-found self confidence. New, different avenues opened up for each of them. John became intensely creative and began to write poetry, while the son, Kevin, who had previously experienced learning difficulties at school, became an A-grade student. John and Elaine gave up smoking and drinking after the encounter, and the whole family gave up eating meat and developed strong feelings on the subject of the environment.

Abductees frequently report that the aliens are here to warn us that humankind is about to destroy the planet with nuclear weapons or our assault on the environment. Such things have been reported by contactees.since the 1950s.

In all these cases the after-effects were real, but no one knows why they happen. Some suggest that the alien presence has had a direct effect on the brain or consciousness of the victim. Others point out that similar changes in people had been observed in the aftermath of harrowing wartime experiences.

Frying Tonight
UFO encounters are best avoided, according to French UFOlogist, Jaques Vallee. He points out that the phenomenon dictates that a large amount of energy must confined in a restricted space. Just

how dangerous this could be to human beings was calculated by American physicist Professor Galloway, who saw a UFO while driving along a highway in Louisiana one night. As he grew closer, the light from the UFO became as powerful as a car's headlights. Knowing the energy emitted by headlights and estimating the distance to the UFO, he was able to work out that the light energy it was emitting was equivalent to the output of a small nuclear reactor.

Dr Edward Condon, who conducted the University of Colorado's UFO investigation for the USAF, checked the figures and confirmed his conclusion.

Duck and Cover

Aliens have also taken a more direct approach in helping humankind to save itself from itself by turning their attentions on nuclear weapons facilities. In the 1950s, when extraterrestrials first contacted humankind, they warned us about nuclear weapons. We took no notice. Since then, they have decided to take the matter into their own hands.

One attack came at the height of the Cold War. On 27 October 1975, the air-raid sirens sounded at Loring Air Force Base in Maine. An unidentified flying object had penetrated the secure air space above the Intercontinental Ballistic Missile (ICBM) installation – one of over two thousand across America that were maintained in a state of constant readiness in case of a Soviet sneak attack. Even though the radar contact had not identified the incoming object as a Soviet missile, the military personnel on the base ran to their emergency stations, ready for the attack that they had spent so long preparing for.

A jet fighter was scrambled to check out the situation. But the pilot, Flight Sergeant Steven Eichner, found that the incoming object was not a Soviet missile. It was something far more exotic. Eichner saw an object that he described as 'a stretched-out football about the length of four trucks, hovering motionless in the air'. It was like nothing he had ever seen before.

It circled around the base for forty minutes then left as quickly as it had arrived. But it returned again the following day. This time it hovered over the base at a height of 160 feet, then landed between two ICBM silos. The military police took charge. They sent vehicles rushing at it in a suicide attack. But instead of retaliating, the UFO shot up into the air and disappeared. The emergency was over, but what no one knew was that this was the beginning of what was to become a sustained campaign of alien intervention at ICBM sites across America.

Sabotage

Just a few weeks after the Loring intrusion, the massive Malmstrom ICBM complex near Lewiston, Montana, played host to a similar but far more baffling UFO encounter. On 7 November, the security alarm sounded, indicating someone had intruded on to the base. The system showed that the problem was in the area of missile silo K-7. A Sabotage Alert Team was despatched. When they reached K-7, they saw a huge disc that was as large as a football field and glowing orange, hovering over the area. As they watched, the UFO sent a beam of light, as brilliant as daylight, down into the silo.

The SAT team was ordered to go in closer but refused. They were armed with machine guns, but none of the team opened fire. Air Force jets went in, but as they neared the object, it vanished. Then when the planes had passed, it suddenly reappeared. Eventually, it shot vertically into the sky until it disappeared from the radar.

A team of technicians was sent down into K-7 to check that everything was okay. They found that the launch and target codes for each of the missiles had been altered. These are the seven-digit codes that prevent the missiles being launched except by direct order from the President. They also fix each missile's target destinations. The codes are the ones that are kept in a black briefcase handcuffed to an officer who always accompanies the Commander in Chief wherever he goes. How these codes came to be altered remains a mystery.

Documents released by Colonel Terence C. James of the North

American Defense Command (NORAD) reveal that, during this period, twenty-four UFO sightings were reported over six different missile silos at Malmstrom. Michael Hesemann investigated the incident in his book *UFOs: The Secret History* and concluded: 'If at that moment an atomic war had broken out, the US would have been helpless. Not one rocket could have been started.'

Defenceless

Such incidents were not confined to Loring AFB and Malmstrom. From 27 October to 19 November 1975, there was a wave of incidents during which UFOs targeted a number of America's ICBM facilities. But it does not seem to have ended there.

On 18 January 1978, several witnesses saw a UFO hovering over McGuire AFB in New Jersey. An MP working for Air Force Security gave chase and found the UFO hovering over his car. Shortly after, the MP saw a three-foot-tall alien, which he said was 'greyish-brown, with a fat head, long arms and a slender body'. He panicked and loosed off five rounds at the alien and one at the UFO hovering above him. The UFO soared vertically and was joined by eleven other craft in the sky.

Afterwards, the body of the alien was found by a runway by a security patrol. A 'bad stench... like ammonia' was coming from it. Later that day, a team from Wright–Patterson came and sprayed the body with chemicals. They then crated it up, loaded it onto a C-141 transport place and left.

Dakota Shoot Out

On 16 November 1977 a UFO encounter took place at Ellsworth Air Force Base in South Dakota, about seven miles south-west of Nisland. A Freedom of Information Act request unearthed the following account:

'At 2059hrs., 16 Nov. 1977, Airmen 1C Phillips, Lt. A. Lims Security Control, telephone WSC. and reported an O2 alarm activation at L-9 and that Lims SAT #1, A-1C Jenkins & A-1C Raeke were dispatched, (Trip #62, ETA 2135hrs.)

'At 2147hrs., A-1C Phillips telephones WSC and reported that the situation at L-9 had been upgraded to a COVERED WAGON PER REQUEST OF Capt. Stokes, Larry D., FSO.

'Security Option 11 was initiated by WSC and Base CSC. BAF (Backup Security Force) #1&&2, were formed. At 2340hrs., 16 Nov. 77, the following information was learned: Upon arrival (2132hrs.) at Site #L-9. LSAT. Jenkins & Raeke, dismounted the SAT vehicle to make a check of the site fence line.

'At this time Raeke observed a bright light shinning vertically upwards from the rear of the fence line of L-9. (There is a small hill approximately 50 yards behind L-9.)

'Jenkins stayed with the SAT vehicle and Raeke proceeded to the source of the light to investigate. As Raeke approached the crest of the hill, he observed an individual dressed in a glowing green metallic uniform and wearing a helmet with visor.

'Raeke immediately challenged the individual, however the individual refused to stop and kept walking towards the rear fence line of L-9. Raeke aimed his M-16 rifle at the intruder and ordered him to stop.

'The intruder turned towards Raeke and aimed an object at Raeke which emitted a bright flash of intense light. The flash of light struck Raeke's M-16 rifle, disintegrating the weapon and causing second and third degree burns to Raeke's hands.

'Raeke immediately took cover and concealment and radioed the situation to Jenkins, who in turn radioed a 10-13 distress to Line Control. Jenkins responded to Raeke's position and carried Raeke back to the SAT vehicle. Jenkins then returned to the rear fence line to stand guard.

'Jenkins observed two intruders dressed in the same uniforms, walk through the rear fence line of L-9. Jenkins challenged the two individuals but they refused to stop. Jenkins aimed and fired two rounds from his M16 rifle.

'One bullet struck one intruder in the back and one bullet struck one intruder in the helmet. Both intruders fell to the ground, however, approximately fifteen seconds later Jenkins had to take cover from a bolt of light that missed him narrowly.

'The two intruders returned to the east side of the hill and disappeared. Jenkins followed the two and observed them go inside a saucer shaped object approximately 20ft in diameter and 20ft thick. The object emitted a glowing greenish light

'Once the intruders were inside, the object climbed vertically upwards and disappeared over the Eastern horizon. BAF> #1 arrived at the site at 2230hrs., and set up a security perimeter. Site Survey Team arrived at the site (0120hrs.) and took radiation readings, which measured from 1.7 to 2.9 roentgens.

'Missile Maintenance examined the missiles and warheads and found the nuclear components missing from the warhead. Col. Speaker, Wing Cmdr. arrived at the site and set up an investigation. A completed follow-up report of this incident will be submitted by order of Col. Speaker.

'Raeke was later treated at the base hospital for second and third degree radiation burns to each hand. Raeke's M-16 rifle could not be located at the site.'

The Soviet Threat

At first the strange alien craft attacking American air bases were thought to be part of the Soviet threat. But the flight characteristics and eyewitness reports from highly trained Air Force observers led the brass to conclude that these were no terrestrial intruders. It was only years later, after the collapse of the Soviet Union, that they discovered that Soviet missile sites also had their hands full with alien intruders: 124 KGB UFO files were released, revealing that Russian nuclear facilities were receiving similar UFO attention.

On 28 June 1988, a UFO was seen by four witnesses flying back and forth over a military base near the nuclear test site of Kapustin Yar in the lowland of the Caspians for two hours. The KGB report said that the UFO flew over the weapons storage area and beamed a shaft of light down into the missile silo. The report fails to mention whether the missiles in the depot were nuclear.

In March 1993, Colonel Boris Sokolov of the Soviet Ministry of Defence told US TV journalist George Knapp that he had been flown to an ICBM base in the Ukraine. On the way, he had been given a top-secret report describing an incident that took place there in October 1983. The report said that a UFO had come close to triggering World War III after it had penetrated Soviet air space and had hovered over the nuclear missile silos. Attempts to shoot the alien craft down had failed when the automatic mechanism for firing the defensive missiles packed up. This was thought to be due to the influence of the UFO. Again the launch codes for the ICBMs had been scrambled, putting that part of the Soviet nuclear arsenal out of action.

Benign Intent

The Russians are now convinced of the aliens' benign intentions. In February 1997, Italian UFO researcher Giorgio Bongiovanni went to the Russian town of Tever to meet a delegation from the Russian military, headed by General Gennadi Reschetnikov of the Air Force Academy. He said: 'The main attention of UFOs is on all of humanity. But above all it has been the US and Russia, since they have the most powerful nuclear reserves in the world. I think this is the reason the aliens are worried.

Reschetnikov is the highest ranking member of the Russian military to confirm the existence of UFOs and he believes that the aliens are particularly interested in the spiritual condition of humankind. He thinks the aliens are curious about human behaviour and, although they influence us for the good, they expect something in return. That something could be the destruction of nuclear weapons.

Balance of Terror

UFO intrusions at nuclear bases on the continental United States and in the former Soviet Union may explain the aliens' evident interest in USAF airbases in the United Kingdom. One of the security policeman at RAF Woodbridge in Suffolk in 1980 says that he was told by Lieutenant Colonel Charles Halt that a UFO had sent down beams of light over the weapons depot that affected a cache of nuclear weapons that were illegally stored there. The Ministry of Defence was highly concerned when tiny holes were discovered, burned through the walls of the depot.

It is interesting that in none of these cases was the UFO misidentified as incoming ICBMs by either the American or Soviet war rooms, prompting a nuclear response that could have resulted in global annihilation. This is because UFO activity had already forced the two sides in the Cold War to improve their communications, according to UFO researcher Colonel Robert O. Dean.

Between 1963 and 1967 Dean was stationed at NATO's Supreme Headquarters of Allied Powers Europe (SHAPE) in Paris. He was allowed access to the war room there, which was officially known as the Supreme Headquarters Operations Center (SHOC). He says that throughout the 1950s and 1960s NATO defence systems regularly tracked large, circular metallic objects flying in formation over Europe. They appeared to be coming from the Soviet bloc and misidentification of UFOs as Soviet missiles came close to triggering a nuclear exchange.

'On three occasions while I was stationed there,' he says, 'SHAPE went to full nuclear alert.'

Along with other senior military personnel, Colonel Robert O. Dean was shown a number of photographs and videotapes depicting aliens while working at SHAPE.

These brushes with nuclear holocaust prompted the commander of SHAPE, General Lemnitzer, to start a three-year, in-depth study of UFOs. He also established a hotline between SHOC and the Warsaw Pact commander. After the hotline was installed, the situation grew less tense. It led to a direct phone line being established between the White House and the Kremlin. So it was UFOs that led to the thawing of the Cold War and the beginning of *détente*.

Alien Activist

UFOs have intervened elsewhere. In 1986 a number of UFOs were seen hovering over a secret nuclear facility that had been built by the Brazilian government to produce weapons-grade plutonium, in violation of international agreements. Prominent UFO researcher Dr Jim Hurtak investigated the case and discovered that the appearance of the UFOs had attracted the attention of the media, which subsequently discovered the nuclear facility. Because it was built in

defiance of treaty commitments, its construction was found uncon-
stitutional and it was closed.

Hurtak believes that events like this show that aliens come with
benevolent intentions. Michael Hesemann also believes it is reasonable to extrapolate that extraterrestrials would intervene if
human belligerence reached a point where annihilation of the planet became inevitable.

But why are the aliens so interested in our well-being? Dr
Hurtak thinks that extraterrestrials are linked with 'ultraterrestri-
als', or higher spiritual forces, who have intervened before at key
moments in history. Indeed, human life on this planet may only be
an experiment that aliens have a vested interest in seeing succeed.

Abduction researcher Dr John Mack often hears the aliens'
views on human nuclear destructive capabilities from his
abductees. He sees their motives for intervention in human affairs
as far less altruistic. 'The survival of man figures large in the well-
being of creatures we haven't yet met,' he says.

UFO researcher Michael Lindemann also believes that nuclear
war on Earth might have untold consequences in other dimensions.
Extraterrestrials normally adopt a hands-off approach that allows
humans to learn by their own mistakes, he says. They only intrude
when it is critically important, not necessarily for their own agenda, but for a larger reason, such as the balance of the cosmos as a
whole.

However, much of the information about UFO interest in
nuclear installations in the West and in the former Soviet Union is
still withheld from the public. It may be some time before we can
fully assess its impact.

Target Brazil

Alien attentions are not always so benign. Sometimes they attack
for no apparent reason. In the late 1970s, they brought their malevolent attentions to bear on the northern Brazilian states of
Maranhao and Para, which together cover an area larger than the
state of California. Throughout the decade, there had been a huge
wave of UFO reports from this area. But these soon turned out to

be no ordinary sighting reports, where the witness sees lights in the sky that perform extraordinary aerobatics before disappearing at an incredible speed. In northern Brazil the UFO fleet had come with hostile intent. Hundreds of thousands of people reported that UFOs fired on them with beams of light. Some people were chased by balls of light that knocked them unconscious and left them with bizarre wounds.

The epicentre of the alien attack was the remote area around the cities of Belem, Sao Luis and Teresina. Manoel Laiva, the mayor of the small town of Pinheiro, estimated that, in just one year, as many as 50,000 people in the area reported UFO sightings. French UFOlogist Jacques Vallee says that UFOs were being seen every night at the peak of the wave in late 1977. Some were seen descending from the sky to hover over houses and probe the interiors with beams of light. Others were seen emerging from the sea, leading to speculation that the aliens had established an underwater base off the coast.

The alien assault was so widespread that it plainly caused the authorities some concern. When amateur UFOlogists turned up to investigate, they found a crack team from the Brazilian Air Force already on the ground. At the time, the Brazilian government would not confirm or deny the attacks, but in July 1987 all was revealed when Brazil's top UFOlogist A.J. Gevaerd interviewed the head of the Air Force team.

Colonel Uyrange Hollanda, who by then had retired, told Gevaerd that the Air Force's top-secret mission to investigate the alien attacks was called 'Operation Saucer'. The investigation began in September 1977 and ran for three months. It had been instigated at the request of the state authorities of Maranhao and Para. They had already begun to investigate hundreds of reports of attacks but soon found they had something on their hands that they were ill equipped to cope with. The civil authorities had sent medical teams out to the remote areas where the reports were coming from. The doctors examined the victims, took statements and sent back their findings. When the civil authorities back in the state capitals read these, they found them so disturbing that they insisted the

Air Force take some sort of action.

Stationed at the headquarters of the 1st Regional Air Command at Belem, Colonel Hollanda was ordered to lead a team into the jungle to investigate. At the time, the frequency of the attacks was at an all-time high. Hollanda's team comprised forty specialists. They were a mixture of civilian and military scientists – doctors, biologists, chemist, physicists and engineers. The team's official mission was to collect eyewitness reports from villagers, ascertain the source of the attacks, and monitor all alien activity using special photographic equipment. Hollanda also had secret orders to attempt to make contact with the aliens to find out what they wanted.

Operation Saucer's primary objective was the island of Colares, just to the north of Belem. The UFO reports were at their peak there. When the UFO team reached the area, they discovered that most of the inhabitants of Colares had fled in panic. Even the schoolteachers, the dentist and the sheriff had turned tail. And they had every reason to flee.

Dr Wellaide Cecin, who was working on the island during the attacks, had treated thirty patients injured by the aliens. Victims had been struck by beams of light that left them with blackened skin, anaemia, loss of hair, inexplicable red patches on the skin, numbness, uncontrollable shaking and puncture wounds. The aliens often attacked after the victims had gone to bed at night. When the beam hit them, they found themselves immobilised and unable to scream. The beam pressed down on their chest like a huge weight and burned them like a cigarette end. Scientists on the Air Force team suggested that the alien energy beam could have been a complex combination of ionising and non-ionising radiation. If such a beam contained pulsed microwaves, it would disrupt the central nervous system, paralysing the victim, cause hallucinations and even affect long-term behaviour.

Aerial observers were deployed each night to film UFO activity. During the first few weeks, they spotted UFOs every other night. They saw balls of light as well as large, structured craft fly directly over their heads. The alien craft did not attack them, but they gradually started moving in closer, as if they were observing the team sent to observe them.

During their investigations, Hollanda's team also encountered large, disc-shaped craft and cylindrical UFOs, as well as much smaller vehicles. Another strange UFO often seen was box shaped. Dubbed the 'flying refrigerator', it made a humming sound that remained at the same pitch despite changes in speed and acceleration.

The balls of light also came in a variety of sizes. When some of these moved close to the Air Force observers, the intensity of their brilliance diminished and the observers were then able to make out the shape of a vehicle inside. They were tear shaped with a transparent canopy, similar to that of a helicopter. Under the canopy a number of alien figures could be seen. The aliens were generally of the classic Grey type, about four feet tall, with big black eyes. Other types were also seen. Hollanda's team took photographs of the craft they encountered, and made a series of sketches of the aliens.

Although the aliens showed no hostile intent towards the Air Force team, their attacks on local hunters and fishermen continued. A variety of craft were involved. Among of the most deadly were large, cylindrical UFOs the villagers called *camburoes*. These would hover over an area and send out powerful beams of light that would sweep back and forth across the ground. One witness, Joao de Brito, related what happened when a friend of his was attacked.

'He felt the light bearing down on his body,' de Brito said, 'and he felt his strength being sucked out of him. He was sure he was going to die. The flying thing was shaped like a cylinder, and he could hear voices coming from it in an unknown language. It left him powerless and he ended up in hospital.'

When the villagers tried to escape the bright beams of light and sheltered in their homes, they found that the alien beams could easily slice through roofs and walls. The local people's only experience of anything similar was the menace of wild animals, so they lit huge fires down by the river and gathered around them. Strangely this seemed to deter the aliens – to begin with. But after a few weeks, they got used to the fires and the attacks resumed.

About seven weeks into Operation Saucer, the UFO activity began to increase dramatically and the aliens appeared more hostile. Each time Hollanda moved his team to a new area of operation, a UFO would already be hovering over their destination when they arrived. This left Hollanda feeling that the aliens were able to read his thoughts and anticipate his every move. He became increasingly aware that his team had become the object of intense scrutiny. In one extraordinary incident, Hollanda and one of his men set off up one of the Amazon tributaries in a small boat. They were about seventy-five miles from Belem when Hollanda decided to return to camp. A sudden storm meant that the rivers in the area were flooding rapidly, making navigation difficult. As they turned a bend in the river, they saw a huge oval-shaped UFO, around three hundred foot tall, hovering over the bank. As they watched, a door slid open at the top of the craft and a figure emerged. It began to float gently towards them. Without his full force around him, Hollanda decided it was time to make a strategic withdrawal, gunned the out-board motor and made a rapid escape.

Although the Air Force team itself had not been attacked, Holland believed that all of them had been abducted. Hollanda believed that he had undergone multiple abductions himself and all the team members reported experiencing periods of 'missing time'. Hollanda himself had a series of strange dreams. These are common in abductees and are often unconscious memories of the abduction experience.

During his interview, Hollanda told Gevaerd that he had been physically and psychologically examined by the aliens. He said this was for some sort of preparation, but he did not know what for. Hollanda even gave Gevaerd a drawing of one of extraterrestrials holding a pistol-shaped device used in the examination.

It was clear that abduction was part of a long-term alien agenda, as abductions from the area had been going on for quite some time. Sixteen-year-old Antonio Alves Ferreira had been first taken on 4 January 1975. He had heard a buzzing sound in the back yard of his parent's house in the Indigo district of Sao Luis. When he went outside to find out what it was, he saw a small disc hovering over the house. He was not alone. Around five hundred other witnesses reported seeing the same UFO. Since the first encounter Ferreira has been abducted eleven times. Three humanoid aliens are responsible. They told him they were from the planet 'Protu'. They made a clone of him to use and left it as a double on Earth, while he was on their craft. He learned their language and, on one occasion, recorded their conversation. This is the only known recording of on alien speech.

Then on 10 July 1977, a chicken farmer from Pinheiro named Jose Benedito Bogea was on his way on foot to Sao Luis when he was pursued by a bright, bluish-green light.

'I raised my arms,' he said, 'and I saw a bright flash of light. It knocked me to the ground. I felt like I'd had an electric shock. Then I passed out.'

When he came too he found himself in a strange alien city with avenues and gardens. Later he was transported back to Earth and dropped off some seventy-five miles from where he had been abducted. He had been missing for twenty-four hours.

Ninety days after Hollanda's team began their investigation, Operation Saucer was suddenly stopped. Hollanda was ordered to close down the operation and forget about it. This was easier said than done as Hollanda continued to feel the effects years after the operation ended. He said he could feel the presence of the aliens in his home. Sometimes he could see them and sometimes he could just feel they were there.

After Operation Saucer, Hollanda also found that he had acquired paranormal abilities. He was able to read people's thoughts. Later he found he could predict the future. He would know in advance that people were about to turn up at his house and he could tell what was going to happen at work.

Despite these fringe benefits, the abduction experience had a profound and disturbing impact on Hollanda. During the interview with Gevaerd he would often break down and cry. His wife became so concerned that she tried to stop the interview. In an effort to help Hollanda come to terms with the experience, Gevaerd arranged regressional hypnosis for Hollanda. But two days before the first session, Hollanda committed suicide. Gevaerd believes that he was the victim of the profound psychological trauma that can be incurred by exposure to extraterrestrials.

Before Hollanda died, he gave Gevaerd copies of a number of documents that had been included in the detailed report he had submitted to the Armed Forces Headquarters in Brasilia. He also gave Gevaerd copies of some of the five hundred photographs the team had taken in the area. After Hollanda submitted his report, he got no response from the authorities and the outcome of Operation Saucer is unknown.

By the early 1980s, the frequency of UFO sightings and alien attacks in the area had dropped significantly, but they have never stopped completely. Gevaerd believes that aliens have selected remote areas in Brazil where they can go about their activities with impunity. The principal agenda behind the attacks, he says, is some form of biological experimentation. Other investigators have come to the same conclusion.

Fighting Back

Human beings are a resilient species. Even in the face of alien aggression we are not going to give up without a fight. Since 1980 and the beginnings of America's 'Stars Wars' programme, weapons have been under development that can shoot alien craft from the skies.

They had one of their first successes on 28 September 1989, when a mysterious object was shot down over Long Island, New York. According to UFO researchers Brian Levin and John Ford of the Long Island UFO Network, the craft was destroyed using a 'Doppler radar system' built by the III Electronics company in con-junction with the Brookhaven National Laboratories, as part of the Strategic Defense Initiative.

Some three years later, on 24 November 1992, a second UFO was downed in the same area. Around 7 p.m., eyewitness Walter Knowles saw what he described as 'a tubular, dark metallic object with blue lights on each end' moving slowly over South Haven Park. Then he saw a blinding flash of light and the spacecraft crashed into the park. John Ford later obtained a video, shot by Brookhaven Fire Fighters, that shows the charred wreckage of the alien ship.

Over recent years, the number of reports of hostile exchanges between the military and UFOs has risen dramatically. It also appears that military attacks on UFOs have been carried out using exotic technology. Many investigators now believe that much of today's military technology, particularly weapons developed for the Strategic Defense Initiative and now the National Missile Defense programme, has been created with the express purpose of repulsing an alien invasion.

Even more remarkable evidence that this is the case comes from a video shot by one of the TV cameras aboard NASA's Space Shuttle *Discovery* on 15 September 1991. It shows number of strange glowing objects entering the picture. They are seen to respond to a series of flashes from Earth, make a ninety-degree turn – something impossible for a terrestrial craft – then accelerate away. The video comes from the US cable TV channel *NASA Select*, which broadcasts continuous coverage of NASA missions.

The so-called 'STS 48' tape has generated enormous controversy and is regularly screened on terrestrial TV. NASA maintains that the glowing objects were nothing more than ice crystals or space debris being moved about by the thrusts of the Shuttle's altitude adjustment rockets. But this has been discredited by Dr Jack Kasher, a physicist at the University of Nebraska, Omaha.

'NASA claimed they were ice crystals. We proved that was physically impossible,' says Kasher. 'Ice crystals couldn't change direction in the way these objects could.'

According his analysis, he estimates that the objects were at the very least ten miles from the Shuttle. He also calculated that they were able to accelerate from zero to 2,500 miles an hour in just one second. If the objects were a hundred miles away, as Kasher believes, in one second they reached over 15,000 miles an hour. This would have subjected the ship to a force of over 1050 Gs – far beyond the capability of any terrestrial craft. However, there have been plenty of sightings of such extraordinary craft before. What

makes the STS 48 video so controversial is that it also shows that
the craft made off at these astonishing speeds because they were
fired on by some exotic weapons system. Careful analysis of the
video shows that a double flash of energy was aimed at one of the
craft. Its response is immediate. It changes direction and acceler-
ates away at incredible speed.

Kasher was employed to work on the Star Wars programme
until 1996. He points out that, despite the huge amounts of money
spent, no anti-ICBM umbrella was ever built. Meanwhile, $35 bil-
lion is spent every year in a 'black budget' to develop all sorts of
covert technologies.

'It is entirely conceivable that what appears to be a weapon firing at the objects in the STS 48 video may, indeed, be the result of
some covert black budget,' he says.

What's more, it backs former Pentagon alien technology expert
Colonel Philip Corso's thesis that the US have been secretly fighting a covert war against the aliens for 50 years. He too believes that
SDI was developed not only to protect against Soviet ICBMs, but
also to defend against alien invaders.

US government policy documents also back Corso's position. In
1967, the National Security Agency – America's largest and most
secret intelligence service – produced a study entitled *UFO
Hypothesis and Survival Questions*. It recommended 'developing
adequate defense measures' against alien invaders. Then in 1978,
Michael Michaud, Deputy Director of the US State Department's
Office of International Security Policy, said: 'Aliens from other
solar systems are a potential threat to us, and we are a potential
threat to them. Even if an alien species had achieved true peace
within its own ranks, it would still be worried about us and would
take the measures it felt were necessary to protect itself. This
includes the possibilities of military action.'

Major General Robert L. Schweitzer, a member of the National
Security Council, was asked to comment. He said: 'President
Reagan is well aware of the threat you document so clearly and is
doing all in his power to restore the national defense margin of
safety as quickly and prudently as possible.'

It was President Reagan who instigated the Star Wars programme.

Under Attack

The modern military's gung-ho attitude could well be because the armed forces themselves have been under attack since flying saucers first appeared in our skies.

One of the earliest hostile encounters occurred over Kentucky on 7 January 1948. Captain Thomas F. Mantell was flying an F-51 Mustang when he was asked to check out reports of a strange flying object. At 2:40 p.m. he made visual contact at 15,000 feet:

'It appears to be metallic, of tremendous size,' he radioed back. 'I'm trying to close for a better look.'

He followed it up to 30,000 feet where, though he was a very experienced pilot, he lost consciousness due to lack of oxygen and crashed. Richard T. Miller was in the operations room at Godman Air Force Base and heard Mantell's last words.

'My God, I see people in this thing,' he said.

It appears he got too close. Witnesses saw the plane being enveloped in white light. It 'belly flopped' onto the ground, but came off remarkably unscathed – seeing that it had just fallen from 30,000 feet. And Miller said that it had crashed more than an hour after its fuel was supposed to have run out.

An eerily similar encounter took place between a military helicopter and a UFO over Ohio in 1973. On 18 October, Captain Lawrence Coyne and his three crew members were approaching Cleveland Hopkins military airport, when they saw a red light approaching them at high speed on a collision course. Coyne took evasive action and tried to put an emergency call through to the control tower, but it was blocked by interference from the alien craft. Then they saw a cigar-shaped UFO, around sixty-five feet in length. It had a domed top with portholes. It sent out a green beam of energy, which enveloped the helicopter.

Coyne shouted: 'My God, what's happening?'

The beam pulled the helicopter upwards, towards the alien craft. Together they ascended at a rate of around 1,500 feet a minute until they reached 5,000 feet. Then the energy beam flicked out, releasing the helicopter, and the UFO took off at tremendous speed. Numerous eyewitnesses saw the encounter. People stopped their cars on the nearby highway to watch. They described how the green light illuminated the entire area.

Another encounter occurred over pre-revolutionary Iran. When the Shah was still in power, Iran was one of the US's staunchest allies and the Iranian Air Force was equipped with the latest American attack aircraft. At around 1 a.m. on 19 September 1976, Iranian military radar operators detected an unidentified object flying at an altitude of six thousand feet over the Merkabah Tower in Tehran. An F-4 Phantom jet was scrambled from Shahrokin Air Force Base to intercept the mysterious craft. As the interceptor jet sped to within twenty-two miles of the object, the aircraft's instrumentation panel suddenly went dead. The pilot tried to report the malfunction, but the communications equipment was also out. He turned, breaking off the intercept and heading back to base. Then, when it presented no further threat to the UFO, the Phantom's systems came back to life.

In the mean time, a second Phantom had been despatched to intercept the UFO. This time, when the jet got within striking distance, the UFO sped off. The Phantom gave chase, but suddenly the pilot saw 'flashing strobe lights arranged in a rectangular pattern' pulsing in front of his face. Even so, the pilot made another attempt to close in on the UFO. This time a brightly-lit object emerged from the UFO and began moving at high speed towards the jet. This was plainly a hostile act. The pilot automatically retaliated with a Sidewinder. But as he tried to activate it, his weapons system went dead and he lost all communications.

The Phantom was now in imminent danger. The pilot jinked and janked, and banked his jet into a steep dive. Looking around to see if he had shaken the bright object that had been fired at him, he saw it circle around and rejoin the UFO. Almost immediately, the pilot's weapons system was reactivated and his communications returned.

The pilot then saw the UFO fire another missile. This one

descended rapidly towards the ground. It made a controlled landing, then cast a brilliant luminescence over an area that the pilot estimated to be around two miles in diameter. While the pilot was watching it, the UFO disappeared.

A fatal encounter took place between the US military and an alien craft above Puerto Rico on 28 December 1988. At 7:45 a.m. hundreds of eyewitnesses saw a huge, metallic-grey, triangular craft, the size of a football field, hovering over Saman Lake in the Cabo Rojo area, which is one of the island's UFO hotspots. 'It was enormous, with many flashing coloured lights,' said eyewitness Wilson Sosa.

Two US Navy F-14 'Tomcats' were scrambled from Roosevelt Road Naval Base to intercept it. When they caught up with it, the alien craft took evasive action. In an attempt to shake them, it spiralled downwards in tight circles. One F-14 nearly collided with the alien craft, but the UFO jinked out of the way. Despite its size, the alien craft was much more manoeuvrable than the Tomcats.

'The jets tried to intercept it three times,' Wilson Sosa said, 'and that's when the UFO slowed down and almost stopped in mid-air.'

Then, in a seemingly suicidal attack, one of the F-14s flew directly at it. The witnesses braced themselves for a collision. Instead, they saw the aircraft disappear as if it had been drawn into the bigger craft. The other F-14 then approached the rear of the craft. It too was swallowed up. Afterwards the huge craft gave out a blinding flash, and split into two smaller triangular ships, which sped away in opposite directions.

Retribution

The aliens may only have been getting their own back. Puerto Rican Professor of Chemistry Calixto Perez said that he examined a dead humanoid being in 1980. It had been killed by Jose Luis 'Chino' Zayas, a Puerto Rican teenage who, with a bunch of friends, had come across a group of small humanoids while exploring the caves at Tetas de Cayey. One of them turned on Zayas and he battered it to death with a stick, stoving its head in. They kept the corpse as a trophy. It was preserved in formaldehyde by a local undertaker.

Later it was seized by officers who said they were attached to NASA, and photographed, before being 'lost' by US officials.

Rules of Engagement

The official policy of the Soviet Air Force was to actively intercept all UFOs and the Russian military established what became the biggest organised effort ever to track and catalogue UFO encounters. Soviet pilots were ordered to get as close to UFOs as possible in an attempt to identify them. However, there were encounters that really scared the authorities. This led to a reversal of policy. Standing orders were issued that pilots should avoid all contact.

Meanwhile, South Africa maintained a 'search and destroy' policy and, in 1990, two South African Mirage FIIG jets, armed with experimental Thor-2 laser cannons, hit a UFO and downed it in the Kalahari desert.

Tony Dodd of Quest was contacted by Captain James Van Greunen, a special investigations intelligence officer with the South African Air Force, who provided Dodd with a small dossier on the case. This contained a report that showed the UFO had been clocked by radar travelling over six thousand miles an hour when it was hit. A special team was sent to the crash site where they found a large silvery disc embedded in the ground. High radiation readings were reported and the craft was carefully shipped back to Valhalla air base.

Once the craft was inside a hangar, a hatchway opened up and out stepped two creatures. They were four feet tall, with grey skin, no body hair, over-large heads and huge slanting eyes. The aliens were taken to a medical unit where they were examined. Passed as fit, they were shipped to Wright–Patterson AFB.

Soon after Van Greunen met Dodd in England, he was ordered home by the South African government. He later fled to Germany where he published his story.

2 Evidence

Photographic Evidence

In the face of official denials, many people refuse to believe in the reality of UFOs and, since the beginning of extraterrestrial visitations, UFOlogists have known that witness reports – no matter how unimpeachable the eyewitness – were not enough. So they have struggled to get convincing evidence on film. The problem is that, in these days of science fiction blockbusters and hi-tech wizardry, almost anything can be faked. The most amazing effects can be produced by even the humblest camera.

'The adage that the camera cannot lie was disproved as soon as it was invented,' says UFO researcher Nick Pope.

The footage showing the alien autopsy and the alien interview were worth hundreds of thousands of pounds. Even a good still picture of a UFO can be worth a lot of money. So no photograph can be taken at face value. It has to be thoroughly investigated by skilled researchers. And even then it might be impossible to prove that the picture is genuine.

In the early days of the UFO sightings, anything went. UFOlogists assumed that if an image looked like a UFO, then it was a UFO. Many photographs of alien 'spaceships' were published in the 1940s and 1950s, fuelling the burgeoning UFO fever. To modern eyes many of these snapshots are obvious, crude fakes made by hanging models from trees or tossing hubcaps in the air. But no one looked too closely. Even fairly dubious pictures were considered good publicity. This naive approach was courting disaster.

The Camera Does Lie

UFOlogy's nemesis came in the form of Alex Birch, a teenage boy from Sheffield. In February 1962, Alex and some friends saw a formation of flying saucers above their garden. Alex succeeded in taking a photograph of the extraterrestrial fleet. Even though no one else in Sheffield had seen the craft, the photograph was taken at face value. Birch and his father were treated like heroes. They were invited to London to file their sighting report in person with officials of the British Air Ministry. And Alex addressed a packed audience at the inaugural meeting of the British UFO Research Association.

Among UFO enthusiasts it was one of the most talked about photographs in years. The problem was that the UFO lobby were so eager to believe that it was genuine that nobody carried out any meaningful investigation. All the picture showed was a smattering of dark blobs on a grainy picture of the sky. Nevertheless, the case entered UFO folklore as an unsolved mystery.

Ten years later, Alex Birch had grown up and he decided to confess. The photograph was a trick. He had painted a few crude flying saucers on to a sheet of glass, propped it up in his back garden

A fake UFO photograph, made in the early 1990s in the former Soviet Union

and photographed it against some blurred tree branches and the sky. To the uncritical eyes, the result vaguely resembled UFOs hovering in mid-air. Cleverly he had avoided including in the shot any reference point, such as a building, which would give the viewer some idea of the size of the objects and their distance from the camera.

Two photographs were taken of a UFO in his garden by Ralph Ditter at Zanesville, Ohio, USA, on 13 November 1966. He later admitted a hoax.

Birch's confession caused a sensation. The general view was that he had set the cause of UFOlogy back years. In fact, in the long run, he probably did it a great service. After his schoolboy hoax, UFO enthusiasts would never be as gullible again. UFO bodies set up guidelines that were to be used when investigating photographic cases. Over the years, these have been constantly refined and improved. These guidelines were used to review old UFO photographs and obvious fakes were thrown up. They also allowed UFOlogists to guard against new hoaxes and helped them weed out what were termed 'accidental fakes'.

Authentication

Just as the human eye can easily be deceived, the camera is open to being fooled. If an eyewitness is willing to believe that a perfectly ordinary light shining through a mist-filled sky is a UFO, a camera will not tell them it's not. In fact, a camera can be a liability when UFO spotting. You experience what you see very differently through the limited frame of a viewfinder than with the naked eye.

Because a camera freezes an instant in a single shot, things that looked quite normal in motion can appear as anomalous in a photograph. A common example of an 'accidental fake' can occur when a bird flies through the scene. For just a fraction of a second that the shutter is open, the bird's wings will be caught in a configuration that would not normally be seen by the human eye. And when that is rendered in the two dimensions of a photographic print, instead of the three dimensions of real life, it might look deceptively like a flying saucer – even if the photographer had no intention of producing a fake.

Calling in a photographic expert is now an automatic first step. They can pick out things like lens flare and other aberrations. In all, around five thousand photographic cases have been investigated around the world and a very small number – perhaps only fifty – really seem to be unexplained. Most are a mixture of accidental fakes, common confusion and out-and-out trickery. Even when visual evidence appears irrefutable, few experts would stake their reputation on a picture being genuine.

'Photographs are poor evidence because there are so many things we can do to technically produce images,' says retired USAF colonel and prominent UFOlogist Wendelle Stevens.

Stevens himself goes to great lengths to authenticate the photographs that are sent to him. He interviews the photographer, visits the place where the pictures were taken and takes his own shots from the same spot to use as a reference. By comparing his picture with the original he can usually work out how big the object is and how far it is from the lens. This eliminates the photographs that have been faked using models.

Another technique Steven employs is an evaluation of the 'blur factor'. The amount of blurring on the object, relative to that of other objects in the picture, helps determine whether the object is moving, and if so, how fast. The approximate speed and direction of flight can also be gauged from the 'edge definition'. This exploits the Doppler effect, where light waves from the leading edge are compressed, while those from the trailing edge are stretched.

The distance of an object from the lens can also be judged by 'atmospheric attenuation'. This is caused by moisture in the atmosphere that cuts down the amount of light reaching the lens. Computer analysis also picks up the 'chroma factor'. As red light is more readily absorbed by the atmosphere than blue, the image should contain a greater component of blue the further it is from the camera.

UFO Down

Winnowing out the accidental fake is never easy. One seemingly cast-iron photograph was only discredited after twenty-three years. In November 1966, a famous scientist was driving across the Williamette Pass in Oregon. He had a camera with him and was planning to take photographs of the snow-decked peaks. But as he was driving, he saw out of the corner of his eye a strange object zipping skywards. Reacting instinctively, he fired off a shot.

When the photograph was developed it showed a flat-bottomed disc climbing from the trees, sucking a plume of snow in its wake. More remarkable still was the fact that three separate images of the UFO were on the one print. It was as if the craft had dematerialised and rematerialised several times during the few hundredths of a second that the camera shutter was open. The cameraman was not certain of what he had seen and wished to remain anonymous. He was a big-name biochemist with a PhD and a reputation to lose, certainly not your average hoaxer. Besides, the photograph seemed to speak for itself.

The impeccable credentials of the photographer did play a part in how seriously the case was taken. *Photographic Magazine* conducted an investigation and gave the picture a clean bill of health. The optical and physical characteristics of the camera and image were even used to deduce the approximate shape, size and speed of the mysterious object.

Then in 1993, researcher Irwin Weider announced that the photo was a fake. Everyone was shocked. For years Weider had believed the photograph really did show a UFO. *Photographic Magazine*'s investigation seemed conclusive. But then Weider had taken a trip through the area where the picture had been taken and thought he saw a UFO himself. He drove up and down the road the same stretch of road and found that the 'UFO' only appeared under very specific conditions. This aroused his suspicion. He began conducting experiments, taking pictures from his moving car and using different shutter speeds. He eventually discovered that the UFO was actually a road sign, which appeared to be a flying saucer due to the interaction of the car and camera. He could even reproduce the triple image at the right speeds.

The world of UFOlogy was stunned by this news, but it just goes to show how carefully photographic evidence must be evaluated. However, Weider's tenacious methods do not always bear fruit.

The Genuine Article

There are some UFO photographs that cannot be dismissed. One such picture was taken by farmer Paul Trent, who snapped a flying saucer over his ranch near McMinnville, Oregon on 11 May 1950. The photograph's background and foreground were both clear, allowing the UFO's size and distance to be estimated. Subsequent computer enhancement has revealed that the disc is solid, between sixty and a hundred feet in diameter, and made from a highly reflective material.

Then on 16 January 1958, when the Brazilian naval vessel *Almirante Saldanha* was carrying a team of scientists to a weather station on Trindade Island – an uninhabited rock in the South Atlantic – a UFO appeared low above the ocean and flew past the ship. It circled the island and headed away. More than a dozen people on the ship saw it. One of them was the expedition photographer. He had his camera to hand and took a sequence of shots clearly showing the object.

When the Brazilian captain got back to port, he had the film processed and the resulting pictures were handed over to the military. The Brazilian military's top photo reconnaissance experts examined them and could find no fault. After some deliberation, the Brazilian government released the film and admitted that they were unable to account for what the pictures showed. As the technology has developed, the Brazilian photographs have been regularly reassessed. Even computer enhancement of the photographs has failed to prove them fakes. Even so, sceptics continue to denounce the photographs as a mirage.

Other convincing pictures have come to light more recently. UFOlogist are surprised that, with the growth of camera ownership, they are not inundated with hoaxing and accidental fakes. However, everyone is now so alert to the possibilities that only the genuine cases get left behind.

In 1983 police officer Tony Dodd photographed a UFO near Addingham in Yorkshire. He sent his negatives and prints to Ground Saucer Watch, a UFO research group. They used computer enhancement and a process called 'density slicing' to analyse the pictures and found that the UFO was above the horizon and air-

A UFO photographed at Trindade Island, South Atlantic Ocean, 16 January 1958.

borne. The grain of the film was analysed using a technique called 'edge enhancement', which confirmed that there was nothing supporting the flying object. GSW identified vapour come from the craft. This vapour trail blended with the atmosphere, convincing investigators that an image of a UFO could not simply have been matted into a picture of the sky. 'Colour contouring' was used to confirm that the UFO was spherical. GSW concluded: 'The UFO appears structured and thirty feet in diameter. This represents Britain's first confirmed UFO photograph.' Sceptics still doubt the evidence of their eyes.

A UFO photographed at Trindade Island, South Atlantic Ocean, 16 January 1958.

Even though it seems to be impossible to find that one piece of clinching photographic evidence, that does not mean that UFO photographs as a whole do not tell their own tale. Dr Bruce Maccabee, an optical physicist for the Surface Weapons division of the US Navy, has been called in to investigate numerous cases. He has seen more UFO photographs than most and he has come to some very clear conclusions.

'I believe that UFOs are real and that they are alien in origin,' he says. 'I have established this through my own research and the study of many years of evidence. Photographic cases are often inconclusive and frustrating for the investigator. That final piece of evidence simply may not be available. However, there are sufficient numbers of impressive cases where it can be established with reasonable conviction that some kind of extraordinary craft was photographed. Such evidence provides a case that demands to be answered by the scientific community.'

The Test of Time

Among the UFO photographs that have stood the test of time are those taken by Paul Villa in New Mexico in the 1960s. They were widely published at the time and UFOlogists believe that they are some of the best ever taken. Even so, there are some puzzling aspects to Villa's story that have caused some sceptics to doubt the evidence of their own eyes.

Villa's story began ten years before he photographed his first series of saucers in 1963. While working for the Department of Water and Power in Los Angeles, he had been contacted by extra-terrestrials. One day in 1953, he was in the Long Beach area when he was overcome with an urge to go down to the beach. There, he met a strange man nearly seven tall. This spooked Villa. He felt afraid and wanted to run away, but then the strange man addressed him by his name and told him many personal things about himself that only the closest of friends would have known. And he could mind-read. At first Villa was puzzled. Then he realised that the being he was talking to was a very superior intelligence – not just a more than averagely intelligent human being but a super-intelligent extraterrestrial.

'He knew everything I had in my mind and told me many things that had taken place in my life,' Villa recalled. 'He then told me to look out beyond the reef. I saw a metallic-looking, disc-shaped object that seemed to be floating on the water. Then the spaceman asked if I would like to go aboard the craft and look around, and I went with him.'

It was too good an opportunity to miss. Once on board the saucer, Villa met other extraterrestrial beings that were human-like in appearance, though 'more refined in face and body'. They had an advanced knowledge of science and explained to him many things that baffled scientists. They told Villa that the galaxy where the Earth resides was just one among an unfathomable number of galaxies that were inhabited across the entire universe – it was a single grain of sand on a vast beach – and that a superior intelligence governed the universe and everything in it. The aliens had bases on the Moon, but their main base was Phobos, one of the two satellites of Mars. Phobos was actually hollow and had been constructed by the aliens. The alien technology was so advanced that their spaceships could penetrate the Earth's airspace without being detected by radar, unless they wanted to call attention to their presence. Alien craft were regularly visiting Earth and the aliens said that more and more sightings were going to take place to increase public awareness of their existence. They then reassured Villa that they had come to Earth on a friendly mission to help humankind.

Born Apolinar Alberto Villa Jr. in 1916, Villa was of mixed Spanish, Native America, Scottish and German descent. He later came to believe that he had been in telepathic communication with aliens since he was five. Although his formal education did not take him beyond tenth grade, he had a mastery of mathematics, physics, electrical engineering and mechanics. He served as an engineer in

A UFO photographed by Paul Villa near Albuquerque, New Mexico, USA, on 16 June 1963, the US Air Force and made his living as a mechanic in civilian life.

Ten years after the Long Beach encounter, on 16 June 1963, Villa was contacted telepathically by aliens. He was told to go to a place near the town of Peralta, New Mexico, about fifteen miles south of Albuquerque. He drove there alone, as instructed, arriving at 2 p.m. Soon after, a flying saucer appeared. It was between 150 and 160 feet in diameter. The ship hovered low in the sky and seemed to pose at various distances so that Villa could get good shots of it. He took a series of photographs. In some of them the craft is framed by the trees, and some show his truck in the foreground. This reference is exactly what photographic experts need if they are going to prove a picture genuine.

When the spacecraft first appeared between the trees, the bottom was glowing amber-red, as if it was red hot. The colours changed to shiny chrome, then to dull aluminium grey, then back to amber. At one point it became so bright it was painful to look at it. When it passed over his head, he could feel the heat it gave off and it gave him a tingling sensation all over his body.

The upper half of the craft was domed and could turn independently from the lower half, though during flight it remained stationary while the lower part rotated. When it did this it gave off a whirring sound like a giant electric motor or a generator. At other times the craft buzzed, or pulsed, or was completely silent. It could do complex aerobatics like flipping onto one edge with its bottom half rotating. The aliens later told him that they did this to demonstrate how they had created an artificial gravity-field within the craft. In such manoeuvres, they remained perfectly comfortable inside.

When the spacecraft hovered over his truck, some three hundred feet up, it caused the truck to rise slowly into the air and float about three feet from the ground for a few minutes. When the craft was about 450 yards away, a flexible probe emerged. It bent into different angles and shapes as it probed the trees and the ground. At the same time, a small, shiny orb came flying out of the spacecraft and disappeared behind trees. It suddenly reappeared, this time glowing red in colour, then shot off at incredible speed. Thoughout the whole display Villa took pictures.

After half an hour, the alien craft landed, settling down on three telescopic legs. Then, through a previously invisible door, five men and four women emerged. They were between seven and ten feet tall and beautiful to look at. They were well proportioned, immaculately groomed and wore tight-fitting, one-piece uniforms. The aliens told Villa that they came from 'the constellation of Coma Berenices, many light years distant'. This did not exactly pinpoint their home. Constellations are only patterns of stars in the sky, as seen from Earth, and Coma Berenices is noted for the large number of galaxies it contains.

Although the aliens were perfectly able to communicate with Villa telepathically, they could also speak many Earth languages. During their conversation, which lasted an hour and a half, they spoke to Villa in both English and Spanish, which was Villa's native tongue. Villa noted that when they talked among themselves they spoke in their own tongue which, to his ears, sounded like 'something akin to Hebrew and Indian'.

They told Villa that the spacecraft they travelled on operated as a mothership for nine remotely controlled monitoring discs. Manoeuvred from instrument panels inside the mothership, they picked up pictures and sound and relayed them back to the television monitor panels. This remote-viewing system was remarkably like the one first seen by George Adamski.

Villa returned to New Mexico in April 1965 to take a second series of photographs. This time the aliens appeared to him in several locations. The best photographs were taken at a place about twenty miles south of Albuquerque on 18 April. Again, when the photographic session was over, the ship settled on its tripod landing gear and the crewmen got out for a chat. This time there were only three of them. They had tanned skin and light brown hair, but they were shorter than the ones he had seen before, only about five feet five inches tall. They talked to Villa nearly two hours, discussing both general topics and personal matters.

A third set of photographs was taken on 19 June 1996. These showed some of the mothership's remotely controlled discs and spheres. The discs were from three to six feet in diameter and were photographed both on the ground and in the air. Often they were surrounded by smaller spheres. Larger discs were also launched from the mothership. Villa estimated that these were some forty feet in diameter. Some of them had flexible, probing antennas, which Villa said resembled the antennae of certain insects – though these are not visible in the photos. But in all his meetings with the aliens, although they would let him photograph their ships, they would not allow him to photograph them.

Villa has other photographs showing one of these remotely controlled discs that he made himself – to the exact specifications given by the aliens. It was about three feet across and was photographed during a test flight being monitored by one of the alien spheres. The disc crashed during the test, due a to slight error that Villa had made. However, the problem was soon rectified.

As it is impossible to distinguish the disc made by Villa from the real alien McCoy, this has been taken as proof that Villa made all of them. However, in none of the photographs is there any hint that the objects are suspended or have been superimposed. Atmospheric 'thickening' – the effect that makes distant objects less well defined than those close to – shows that the objects are not models. William Sherwood, formerly an optical physicist for Eastman-Kodak, studied all the Villa photographs and said they are genuine.

Because his pictures were so widely published in the 1960s, Villa was accused of making a fortune from them. He did not. In fact, he spent his own money sending out free copies. He also spent much of his free time writing to world leaders about what the aliens meant to mankind. In 1967, Ben Blaza of UFO International asked Villa's permission to copyright the photographs. Villa granted it, but made very little money himself.

Nor was Villa an attention seeker. His shunned publicity and rarely granted interviews to the media. He has also been threatened. Helicopters seem to follow him and he has been shot at.

British UFOlogist Timothy Good followed up on the Paul Villa case. In correspondence, Good pointed out the inaccuracies in certain prophecies the aliens had made. The aliens had said that seventeen nations would have the atomic bomb by 1966 – there were probably no more than ten by the year 2000. They said that Ronald Reagan would be elected president in 1976, though he did not make it to the White House until four years later. Worse, they said that there were 'canals' and 'pumping stations' on Mars, and that 'cacti and other plants' grew in certain locations on the red planet.

When asked whether the aliens had lied to him, Villa said no, they just did not tell the whole truth. 'Why should they? People would just make money from that info. Besides, how can humanity appreciate anything if it is beyond their capacity to understand?' he said.

Villa told Good that Walt Disney Studios and the US Air Force had both studied his negatives and found no fault in them. According to Villa, Dr Edward Condon, who headed the University of Colorado's USAF-sponsored investigation team that studied UFOs from 1966 to 1968, said they were the best pictures he had ever seen. But Good could find no mention of Villa or his photographs in Dr Condon's book *Scientific Study of Unidentified Flying Objects*.

In 1976, Villa drove Good around the locations near Albuquerque where he had photographed the alien craft and met their crews. At one of them, Good asked Villa what the other crew members were doing while he was talking to the alien he assumed was the pilot. 'Oh, they were just bathing their feet in the river,' he replied without batting an eyelid.

Like William Sherwood and other researchers who met Villa, Good was impressed and concluded that there was something to his story. Paul Villa died of cancer in 1981.

Scientist's Sightings

Strange lights were seen in the sky over Lubbock, Texas, on the night of 25 August 1951. They were witnessed by an Atomic Energy Commission executive and his wife from their back yard and simultaneously observed by four respected Texas scientists from their vantage point in another part of town.

Approximately three dozen bluish lights were seen. They had

the appearance of a giant flying wing, which moved back and forth across the night skies. Several hundred people in the area witnessed the same phenomenon over the next several days.

On 31 August, Carl Hart Jr. photographed the lights, but photo analysis could not prove Hart's pictures were genuine.

Single Exposure

On 24 May 1964, Jim Templeton, a fireman from Carlisle in the North of England, took his young daughter out to the marches overlooking the Solway Firth to take some photographs. Nothing untoward happened, although both he and his wife noticed an unusual aura in the atmosphere. There was a kind of electric charge in the air, though no storm came. Even nearby cows seemed upset by it.

Some days later, Mr Templeton got his photographs processed by the chemist, who said that it was a pity that the man who had walked past had spoilt the best shot of Elizabeth holding a bunch of flowers. Jim was puzzled. There had been nobody else on the marshes nearby at the time. But sure enough, on the picture in question there was a figure in a silvery white space suit projecting at an odd angle into the air behind the girl's back, as if an unwanted snooper had wrecked the shot.

The case was reported to the police and taken up by Kodak, the film manufacturers, who offered free film for life to anyone who could solve the mystery when their experts failed. It was not, as the police at first guessed, a simple double exposure with one negative accidentally printed on top of another during processing. It was, as Chief Superintendent Oldcorn quickly concluded, just 'one of those things... a freak picture'.

A few weeks later Jim Templeton received two mysterious visitors. He had never heard of 'Men in Black' – they were almost unknown in Britain at that time. But the two men who came to his house in a large Jaguar car wore dark suits and otherwise looked normal. The weird thing about them was their behaviour. They only referred to one another by numbers and asked the most unusual questions as they drove Jim out to the marshes. They wanted to know in minute detail about the weather on the day of the photograph, the activities of local bird life and odd asides like that. Then they tried to make him admit that he had just photographed an ordinary man walking past. Jim responded politely, but rejected this suggestion. At this point, they became angry, got back into the car and drove off leaving him there. He then had to walk five miles across country to get home.

Polaroids

Another alien contactee who could back his story with photographic evidence was sign painter Howard Menger, whose alien encounters began in 1932. His alien contacts came from Venus and demonstrated super-human abilities. At 1 a.m. on 2 August 1956, he snapped a series of Polaroids showing a spacecraft landing and a 'Venusian' getting out. The creature had broad shoulders, a slim waist, long, straight legs and long, blonde hair that blew in the soft warm summer breeze. However, Polaroid photography was in its infancy and the photographs are vague and indistinct. Menger only managed to catch the creature in silhouette against the glowing spacecraft. However, Menger explained that the blurring effect around the figure was caused by the electromagnetic flux surrounding the craft.

Menger later found himself employed by the extraterrestrials to help them learn human ways. He had to cut their hair into Earthly styles and introduce the aliens to Earth food. In return, they took him on trips to the Moon. Unfortunately, his photographs of the Moon came out no better than his portraits of the aliens.

Carroll Wayne Watts, a cotton farmer in Loco, Texas, managed to get some Polaroids of the aliens who abducted him in April 1967. As usual, Watts was stripped naked and examined. Just as he was getting dressed, he tried to steal an alien paperweight. He was alone in the room when he pocketed the two-inch-long piece of metal. Nevertheless, one of his captors came marching in, reached into his pocket and removed the paperweight. Watts was then knocked unconscious.

Polaroid shots of aliens served Police Chief Jeff Greenhaw little better. At 10 p.m. on the night of 17 October 1973, Greenhaw received a call from a woman reporting that a flying saucer had landed in a field near Falkville, Alabama. There, Greenhaw encountered a seven-foot-tall metallic humanoid. He tried to communicate with it, but got no response. But he did manage to snap a series of Polaroids before the alien fled – its huge steps allowed it to easily outplace Greenhaw's patrol car.

'He was running faster than anything I ever saw,' said Greenhaw.

The pictures clearly show the outline of a metallic creature. With his position as chief of police on the line, Greenhaw had no reason to fake the photographs, so his evidence had to be taken seriously. His pictures certainly bought him no money and no fame. Within two weeks of the encounter, an arson attack on his house destroyed the original prints, he began receiving threatening phone calls, his car blew up mysteriously and his wife walked out on him. The pictures brought him unwanted publicity. It was said that he had been

Photograph taken by UFO contactee Howard Menger some time during 1957-8: shows alleged spacewomen walking towards Menger.

duped by a prankster wrapped in silver foil and he was forced to resign as police chief. This was hardly the action of a hoaxer.

Polaroids were also unlucky for twenty-three-year-old Filiberto Caponi. Over a couple of months beginning in May 1993, he had taken a series of photos of an extraterrestrial creature in his home town of Ascoli Piceno. He had found it in a sack, but in subsequent shots the sack was gone and the creature seems to have undergone some type of physical development or growth. At first Caponi thought he had stumbled onto some form of bizarre genetic experiment.

In November 1993, his Polaroids were broadcast on the Italian TV station RAI-DUE. Soon after, the Italian police took Caponi in for questioning. He was charged with 'creating panic'. The police confiscated the photographs and he was forced to sign a confession saying he had faked the whole thing.

Big-Nosed Greys

Former US Navy petty officer Milton had access to the famous Grudge/Blue Book Special Report 13 on UFOs, which the US government claims never existed. He also saw a file belonging to Majestic-12, President Truman's secret commission set up to investigate UFOs, while he was a quartermaster under the Commander in Chief of the Pacific Fleet. In the files, Cooper saw a series of photographs of 'big-nosed Greys'. These creatures had struck a deal with the US government. They came from a dying planet that orbited Betelgeuse. Led by His Omnipotent Highness Krill, they had chosen Earth as their new home. The deal was that, in exchange for alien technological secrets, they would be allowed to share the planet and abduct humans occasionally for experimentation. Unfortunately, the deal soon broke down and the aliens went on an abduction spree. But the treaty was patched up and remains in operation to this day.

Undisputed Evidence

On the night of 2 August 1965 fourteen-year-old Alan Smith saw a UFO from his back garden. It changed colour from white to red

then to green. The quick-thinking teenager got a camera and photographed the object. He sent the image to the USAF investigation
team, who were known as Project Blue Book. They passed it on to
the USAF Photo Analysis Division. The analysts concluded that
the object was a mile from the camera and thirty feet in diameter.
However, in an attempt to debunk the sighting, the report on the
photograph concluded that it could have been made by photo-
graphing 'a multi-colored revolving filter flood-light'. Twenty-one
years later the America UFO group Ground Saucer Watch subjected it to computer analysis which confirmed that it showed 'an
extraordinary flying craft of large dimensions'.

Moving Pictures

While it is relatively easy to fake photographs – or produce fakes
by accident – it is much harder to falsify moving pictures. Although
fifty years ago home movie cameras were comparatively rare, with
the advent of video, there has been huge increase in home movie
making. These days video cameras are often on hand during UFO
sightings and video footage has provided some of the best evidence
that UFOs are actually structured flying vehicles, produced by an
extremely advanced and non-terrestrial technology.

Despite the abundance of excellent footage in the UFO archives,
a film or video fails to carry any real weight unless it has been
subjected to a rigorous series of tests. The most exacting professional analysis is extremely expensive though, so it is only possible to submit a small proportion of movie material for specialist
examination.

Over the years new technology had provided ways of testing
photographs undreamed of when early UFO images were made.
NASA has developed powerful computer programs that can rebuild
images sent back bit by bit from cameras deep in space. The pictures are scanned electronically then sent to Earth as radio waves.
On the way they get mixed up with other electromagnetic radiation.
Atmospheric interference further degrades the signal, but when the
incoming data stream is picked up on Earth, NASA's computer programmes can rebuilt the original and enhance and sharpen the

image. When this technology is applied to ordinary photographs, film and video, it can reveal the most sophisticated trickery. As researchers have become vigilant, the number of UFO photos and video submitted for scrutiny has tumbled.

One of the world's leading experts in UFO film and video analysis is Jim Dilettoso. He has been doing this kind of work since 1977, when he was approached by UFO researcher retired USAF Colonel Wendell Stevens who asked him to look at footage from the controversial Meier case. Stevens chose Dilettoso because he had a background in optical special effects and the latest image processing techniques. With these skills at his command, he pioneered many of the analytical tools that are currently in use to scrutinise UFO footage.

Dilettoso's company – Village Labs of Phoenix, Arizona – is packed with sophisticated equipment. It owns a number of Cray supercomputers along with the most powerful graphics-generating system ever constructed. As well as analysing UFO films, Village Labs uses this equipment to carry out image analysis work for NASA and make the latest specials for Hollywood.

Technology and the procedures Dilettoso has developed over some twenty-five years in the business aside, some footage still passes muster. One video that got the Dilettoso seal of approval

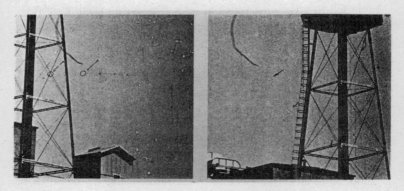

Two frames from a film of UFOs, made on 15 August 1950 at Great Falls, Montana, USA, by Nicholas Mariana.

was shot by Tim Edwards in August 1995. Edwards was out in the back yard of his home in Selida, Colorado, with his daughter when he saw a large cylindrical UFO hovering in the sky. He got his Hi-8 video camera and filmed it continuously until it disappeared, shooting six minutes in all.

The footage eventually found its way to Dilettoso, who started the laborious process of analysis. When reviewing video or film footage, the job of the analysts is to look for evidence of fakery. There are two principal ways a hoax can be perpetrated these days. It can be done in the old-fashioned way using models, or, these days, an image can be produced digitally by computer.

Discovering if an image has been generated by computer is relatively easy. The first thing Dilettoso does is examine the 'vertical interval' – the black bar that divides one video frame from the next. This acts like a fingerprint, with each video machine producing a vertical interval with slightly different characteristics. Obviously if the footage has been shot on one camera in a continuous sequence, all the vertical intervals will be the same. But if the image has been created digitally or edited by a computer the vertical interval will be altered in the process. If this shows that the footage has been interfered with, Dilettoso looks for evidence that an image has been 'gen-locked'. This is a movie technique whereby one image is superimposed on top of another.

Discovering if a model has been used is far more difficult. The only way to do this is to try and calculate the object's size and distance from the camera. Dilettoso then makes an estimate of its direction of flight and its speed. Taking all these things together should tell you whether the object is small enough to be a model. If possible, Dilettoso likes to go to the location where the footage was shot. Then he shoots a tape on the same camera to use as reference.

In the case of the Edwards' tape, it was easily enough to fly up to Colorado and visit Edwards' backyard. Dilettoso was able to shoot from the same position as Edwards, using Edwards' Hi-8. The process of analysis was made easier because Edwards was standing under the eaves of his house when he shot the video. The camera was pointing upwards so the guttering appeared in the foreground. This was key to Dilettoso's analysis.

'When we survey the unknown, we need to know what the characteristics of the known are,' he says.

Dilettoso could measure the dimensions of the gutter and the distance of the camera from it. He could also establish the brightness of the sun reflecting off other surfaces nearby. Dilettoso then used a computer to create a database from the original footage. He located the darkest object in the shot and the brightest. Then he created a scale showing the relative shades of luminosity of those in between. It was then possible to calculate the approximate distance to the UFO, using the intensity of the reflected light as reference. The quality of reflected light from a large object high in the sky is very different from that reflected from a model a few feet from the lens. This provides a basic test to decide if UFO footage is a fake.

When it has been established that an object is large and some distance from the camera it is then necessary to establish whether it is under intelligent control and not a cloud or some other windborne phenomenon. To do this, Dilettoso examines the 'motion blur' of the image. By examining the small differences in the clarity of different parts of an image, it is possible to tell which way the craft is moving and how fast. This must match the speed and direction worked out from the footage as a whole. The motion blur also helps an expert tell whether it is the object that is moving or the camera.

The Edwards footage passed all these tests with flying colours. Dilettoso's conclusion was that the object shown in the video was not a model and was not computer generated. But the really startling result was Dilettoso's estimate of its size. He reckoned that Edwards' UFO was between half-a-mile and a mile in length.

In such convincing cases, UFO researchers ask for a second opinion. In the Edwards' case, the tape was sent to Dr Bruce Maccabee. He agreed that it was not a model but estimated that the object was only between four hundred and eight hundred feet long. 'This was close enough to our estimate to say we were in general agreement,' said Dilettoso.

Case Unsolved

In Britain other footage has withstood the most rigorous examination. On 13 March 1993 Stephen Woolhouse saw a bright light in the sky that drifted silently over farmland behind his house in Bispham, Lancashire. He had a video camera to hand. It was loaded with tape and ready to roll. He filmed the glowing object before it was swallowed up by the darkening skies. The tape was examined by experts from the Northern Anomalies Research Organisation, which confirmed that it showed a flying object. It was neither an airship nor a helicopter according to local air-traffic control. It had no flashing navigation lights and Woolhouse's house was sixteen miles from the nearest airfield. The case remains unsolved.

But in 1996 a spectacular video was released that shows a ball of light creating a crop circle in Wiltshire. A year later evidence was found that indicated that the video was not genuine, merely a sophisticated piece of computerised trickery. But uncovering the hoax took a great deal of time and skill.

Birds on the Wing

At 11:10 a.m. on 2 July 1950 Warrant Officer Delbert C. Newhouse, a veteran Navy photographer, shot about thirty feet of film of ten or twelve strange, silvery objects in the sky near Trementon, Utah. As the objects flew in a westerly direction, one of them veered off from the main group and reversed its course.

After a thousand hours of investigation of the Newhouse film, the Navy Photographic Interpretation laboratory concluded that the objects filmed were not aircraft, birds, balloons or reflections, but were in fact 'self-luminous'.

The 'Robertson Panel' – five distinguished non-military scientists convened by the CIA in 1952 to discredit UFO sightings – concluded otherwise. They decided the objects were a formation of birds reflecting the strong sunlight.

Just Jets

At 11:25 a.m. on 5 August 1950, in Great Falls, Montana, Nicholas Mariana shot nearly twenty seconds of film of two disc-shaped objects as they moved across the sky.

On some of the 250 frames, the objects are seen passing behind the girders of a water tower, which gave film analysts an opportunity to measure the objects' approximate altitude, speed, azimuth, distance and size. It was also a sequence that would have been very difficult to have faked.

Mariana admitted that he had seen two jet fighters on their final approach to a nearby Air Force base just prior to his sighting of the objects, but insisted he knew the difference between the jets and the objects.

The Robertson Panel decided that Mariana did not know the difference – that he had filmed the jets.

The Norfolk Footage

Some of the best UFO footage ever taken was shot in 1997 when Norfolk became a centre of UFO activity. Weird flashing lights were seen in the night sky. Huge cylindrical motherships were floating aloft. And during the day, even when it was clear and sunny, menacing black triangular craft performed seemingly impossible, high-G manoeuvres silently above the broads. Similar sightings had been reported around the world in the 1990s, but what made the Norfolk sightings significant was that they were filmed.

While being open-minded on the subject, David Spoor, a long-time resident of Aulton Broad near Lowestoft in Norfolk, had no interest in UFOs. Then on 19 August 1997, when he was pottering in his back garden, he spotted a cigar-shaped object with a strange strobe light flashing around it in the sky.

'It was a white, self-illuminated cylindrical craft,' says Spoor, 'high in the sky and travelling silently west to east. It seemed to be ringed by bright strobe lights, which flashed randomly but weren't attached to the body of the craft.'

He reckoned that it was forty or fifty feet across, though it was hard to estimate because he could not tell accurately how far it was away. At first it was stationary, then it travelled across the sky at around forty to fifty miles an hour.

As luck would have it, Spoor had recently borrowed a video camera from a friend. He rushed inside to get it. Then, camera in hand, he filmed the UFO as it sailed silently across the sky. Unlike so much UFO footage, the resulting film was clear and unmistakable. But Spoor's coup did not end there. This was just the first of a series of films that would soon make him the Cecil B. De Mille of the UFO world.

In January 1998 he filmed blue beams of light coming at him across a field on the Suffolk border. He could not tell where they were coming from. On 2 February 1998 he shot a number of luminous orbs travelling slowly and silently across the sky. On other occasions he filmed other objects making high-speed manoeuvres that would have generated G-forces no human pilot could withstand. And he filmed numerous black triangles, flying in formation.

Like many people who have seen UFOs, Spoor found his life turned upside down. His house seemed to become the focus for strange forces. Keys bent and twisted in the locks. Lights switched themselves on and off without rhyme or reason. And, most sinisterly, at night, the family's bedrooms were lit up by bright lights which appeared to hover above their yard. Spoor's response was sanguine. He bought a video camera and made his own survey of the skies. Although at first he had questioned his own sanity, by the end of the year, he had shot nearly three hours of footage showing UFO activity over Norfolk. These were backed by his own accounts of the sightings.

Naturally he wanted to find out whether others had witnessed the same thing. A quick check of the local papers told him that others were reporting the odd UFO sighting, but nothing on the scale he had witnessed. However, he made discreet enquiries and found that he was not alone. Another man in the vicinity had also noticed the intense aerial activity. His name was Peter Wrigglesworth. He, too, had filmed the UFOs and had taken his footage to well-known Norfolk UFOlogist David Dane.

Dane was impressed with Wrigglesworth's film and, making enquiries of his own, Dane discovered Spoor and introduced him to Wrigglesworth. This was to become the one of the most productive partnerships in British UFOlogy.

The hours of footage that Wrigglesworth and Spoor had shot was viewed by numerous experts in the field. A number of movie and TV companies in America approached them. At a UFO conference in Laughlin, Nevada, the editor of *UFO* magazine Graham Birdsall offered to authenticate their film for them. He was impressed.

'The object certainly does not conform to any known aerial craft, largely because of the strobe-like features around it,' said Birdsall.

America's leading UFO investigation organisation Quest International had the computer analyst Russell Callahan look at the footage, but he made little progress with Spoor's original film because, apart from the UFO, there was nothing else in the shot to use as a point of reference. For Birdsall this was not a problem.

'All the computer analysis in the world won't tell us where it's from,' he said.

As the UFOlogist most closely involved in the case, Dane, too, believes that the craft are of extraterrestrial origin.

'In all my thirty years' experience of UFOlogy,' he said, 'I've never come across anything quite like this. I still have difficulty taking it in. It is without doubt the best UFO footage I've ever seen.'

Other UFOlogists who have seen the videos are equally enthusiastic, though researcher George Wingfield urges scepticism.

'Something pretty strange is definitely going on above Norfolk,' he said. 'But what it is is another matter. The two men seem genuine and sincere, but that doesn't necessarily mean they're filming what they think they're filming.'

Some have even suggested that the object Spoor filmed on 7 December 1997 was in fact Venus. The planet was visible that night, but it was on the other side of the sky. Others say that Wrigglesworth and Spoor may have filmed aircraft – perhaps experimental ones. The RAF bases at Wattisham, Coltishall, Honington and Marham are nearby. While it is possible that the Jaguars, Tornadoes, air-sea rescue helicopters and conventional military aircraft stationed there may explain some of the sightings in the area, experts say they do not account for all of the objects filmed by Wrigglesworth and Spoor.

In an effort to get to the bottom of the mystery, Dane showed some of the footage to Paul Beaver, a pilot and aeronautical expert who writes for the top military aircraft magazine Jane's *International Defence Review*. At first, he was sceptical.

'My first thoughts were that some of the footage was of kites, or models,' he said, 'but in one sequence, where two black wedge-shape craft are carrying out incredible manoeuvres, I felt that they were more likely RPVs [remotely piloted vehicles] or UAVs [unmanned aerial vehicles] – largely because of their size and the G-forces involved. I wouldn't put it past the military in these areas to be involved in UAV research.'

The RAF said that none of the bases in the vicinity were testing UAVs, but a spokesman at RAF Coltishall explained that, even if they were testing top-secret aircraft, they would obviously refuse to tell anyone. He said that the military carried out very little night flying in the Norfolk area, though, and would offer no opinion on what the craft Wrigglesworth and Spoor had filmed were. But the MoD were adamant.

'No UFOs have penetrated UK airspace, and nothing has been picked up by our detectors,' they said.

Although both Twentieth Century Fox and the BBC have expressed an interest in buying the footage, Wrigglesworth and Spoor have rejected their offers. They say they do not feel that this valuable footage should be exploited for financial gain and they fear that they would be become the centre of a media circus.

'This footage represents the ultimate media scoop, and a lot of people in a position to broadcast it will come away considerably richer for the privilege,' says Dane who is acting as agent for the film. 'Although none of us are "in it for the money", we do want credit to go where it's due. I am not prepared to let footage or individual stills fall into the wrong hands as I believe the whole episode would quickly degenerate into a circus.'

But this stance – however honourable – leaves Wrigglesworth and Spoor open to the charge that they are afraid to open themselves up to proper scrutiny.

Radar Contact

Although photograph and film can be faked, the evidence of trusted and experienced observers is hard to refute. So how can the evidence of highly trained air traffic controllers and military radar operators be dismissed when they see an unidentified blip flashing across their screens?

In the early hours of 21 December 1978 the crew of a Safe Air cargo plane en route from Blenheim to Dunedin, in New Zealand, were requested to search for some explanation for the unusual radar returns that were being tracked at Wellington Airport. Air traffic controller John Gordy said that the targets on his radar screen were unlike any he had ever seen before. As Captain Vern Powell flew his Argosy into the area over New Zealand's South Island, he saw several strange lights. They followed his aircraft for just over eleven miles along the coast before they disappeared. Captain John Randle, also flying an Argosy, on the same route, also diverted into the area and reported seeing UFOs. And at Wellington they were going crazy.

'At one stage our radar controllers had five very strong radar targets where nothing should have been,' said the head of Air Traffic Services at Wellington.

When the Australian TV Channel O from Melbourne heard of this sighting and others in the area, they contacted one of their reporters who happened to be on holiday nearby. The reporter's name was Quentin Fogarty and, when the TV company gave him the details of the sightings, Fogarty jumped at the assignment. He began his report by interviewing the UFO witnesses. Then he persuaded Safe Air to fly him along the same route to film background footage for the programme on the night of 30–31 December, this time in an Argosy flown by Captain Bill Startup.

Fogarty got lucky. Once again, radar picked up the strange returns. At 12:10 a.m., the crew were filming in the aircraft's loading bay when suddenly they saw a number of strange lights in the direction of Kaikoura on South Island.

They radioed Wellington control for information and were told: 'There are targets in your ten o'clock position at thirteen miles appearing and disappearing, not showing at present, but they were a minute ago.' For some time after that, Wellington radar detected a series of targets that came within five miles of the plane.

At 12:22 a.m., the crew were able to correlate both a visual sighting and a radar contact. A formation of six mysterious lights formed up alongside the plane. 'Let's hope they're friendly,' said Fogarty as he trained the TV camera on the UFOs. They seemed to be around a hundred feet in length and the bright lights seemed to be coming from their domed cabins.

Several seconds of film were shot of the UFOs. During the rest of the flight various other targets were seen and also confirmed by radar. On the return flight, more sightings were made, and more footage was shot of what Fogarty described as 'a sort of bell shape with a bright bottom and a less bright top'. As the flight continued, there were further sightings, again confirmed by radar.

Photographic expert Dr Bruce Maccabee flew out from Washington to New Zealand to study the footage. Maccabee was soon convinced that Fogarty had recorded something truly inexplicable and the Wellington case is widely regarded as one of the most convincing in UFO history.

Nevertheless the sightings have remained controversial, even though they were confirmed by radar. Sceptics have attempted to dismiss Fogarty's pictures as anything from the stars, Venus or Jupiter to the moonlight reflecting off a cabbage patch, and even, somewhat bizarrely, Japanese squid boats. But the air crew, who flew that route regularly, know they saw something extraordinary. Fogarty remains completely baffled by what he encountered that night. And the air traffic controllers are convinced that something strange was out there – something that deserved the official tag 'UFO'.

Bogeys over Washington

There can surely be no more famous case of radar-detected sightings than those that occurred over Washington, D.C. in 1952. The huge number of radar contacts caused consternation in military circles. Even the US government's own UFO investigation project feared an alien invasion.

The sightings took place over three consecutive weekends: 19–20 July, 26–27 July and 2–3 August. Around 11:40 p.m. on 19 July, Edward Nugent, an air traffic controller at Washington National Airport, spotted seven unidentified blips on his radar screen. They were around twenty-five miles south-west of the city and travelling at around a hundred miles an hour. Over the next few hours, two radar stations covering the airspace above Washington, D.C. detected eight UFOs in the restricted area around the Capitol building and the White House. For security reasons no civil or military planes are allowed to fly through that restricted zone without special orders. But the UFOs took no notice of that. They were moving so fast that their time within the restricted zone passed in the blinking of an eye. They could accelerate to astonishing speeds, stop dead and turn on a sixpence. These anomalous blips appeared on the capital's radar screens throughout the night and into the early hours of the morning and were confirmed by the sightings of pilots and ground observers.

At 3 a.m., two USAF F-94 Lock Starfire all-weather jet fighters were sent up from Newcastle Air Force Base in nearby Delaware. But when they got airborne, the UFOs simply disappeared, only to return again when the jets had landed. The last one left the capital's radar screens at 5:30 a.m.

The alien fleet turned up again the following weekend. They were first spotted by a National Airlines pilot who saw several of them flying high above his aircraft. He described them as looking like the 'glow of a cigarette'. Again, they were picked up on radar and seen by observers on the ground and in the air. At 11 p.m., two Starfires were scrambled from Newcastle AFB, but again the objects disappeared as the jets closed in and reappeared after they left. However, when a second wave of interceptors went in, the

UFOs remained where they were and the USAF pilots were able to make visual contact with four of them. One of the pilots, Lieutenant William Patterson, reported the UFOs closing on him rapidly. He was surrounded by blue lights, but they fled before he got permission to attack them.

Civil airline pilots also saw the UFOs. Captain S. Pierman of Capital Airlines was one of several who gave visual confirmation of the radar contacts. But the moment he reported his sighting by radio, the object shot away at an incredible speed.

'In all my years of flying I have seen a lot of falling or shooting stars – whatever you call them,' said Captain Pierman. 'But these were much faster than anything I have ever seen. They couldn't have been aircraft. They were moving too fast for that.'

Air traffic control had seen the UFO's extraordinary retreat too. 'It was almost as if whatever controlled it had heard us, or had seen Pierman head toward it,' said Harry Barnes, the senior air traffic controller that night.

Many people came forward with explanations. Some suggested that the radar contacts were simple radar errors or temperature inversions, where pockets of increased temperature in the lower levels of the atmosphere can cause anomalous radar reflections. To explain the pilots' visual corroboration, it was said that the excitement of the radar flap led them to mistake normal lights for UFOs. But these explanations ignore the fact that the pilots' sightings corresponded exactly to the behaviour of the radar contacts.

Leading UFO researcher Don Ecker has led the investigation into the Washington flap and remains convinced that it presents some of the most important evidence in UFO history. Ecker had discovered that it was not only both civil and military pilots who visually confirmed the radar contacts.

'They were witnessed by some of the radar operators that literally left their scopes and went outside and looked physically into the sky,' he says.

He has also dismissed the idea that the contacts could have come from temperature inversions.

'The radar operators were skilled personnel,' he says. 'They were responsible, literally, for bringing in, and having go out, tens of thousands of air travellers every day. The military radar experts were depended upon to keep our skies safe from enemy intrusions, and these guys had, beyond any shadow of a doubt, dealt with things like temperature inversions.'

Ecker also discovered a cover-up. Edward J. Ruppelt was head of Project Blue Book, the US Air Force's official UFO investigation and as such was the man charged with investigating the flap. But when he looked into the case, he found the authorities less than forthcoming. Ruppelt discovered that the authorities 'were going to great extremes and lengths to get this swept under the rug as soon as possible,' says Ecker.

As the Air Force refused to give information to its own UFO investigator, Ruppelt had to turn to the press. He was bitter about being sidelined and, when asked what the Air Force was doing about UFOs entering restricted airspace, he commented: 'I have no idea what the Air Force is doing; in all probability it's doing nothing.'

Major Donald Keyhoe, who would later become a founder member of the National Investigations Committee on Aerial Phenomena (NICAP), was also involved in the investigation. *True* magazine published his analysis of the sightings in 1953, under the title 'What Radar Tells Us About Flying Saucers'.

In the article, Keyhoe shows just how seriously the Pentagon took the sightings by citing remarks made by Director of Operations Major General Roger S. Ramey at the time.

'The Air Force, in compliance with its mission of air defence of the United States, must assume responsibility for the investigation of any object or phenomena in the air over the United States,' Ramey said. 'Fighter units have been instructed to investigate any object observed or established as existing by radar tracks, and to intercept any airborne object identified as hostile or showing hostile interest. This should not be interpreted to mean that air-defence pilots have been instructed to fire haphazardly on anything that flies.'

Ramey's remarks demonstrate that the Air Force believed that the radar contacts were very real. Again Keyhoe pointed out that the radar operators would have been very familiar with false returns, such as temperature inversions. Nevertheless they felt that the blips required further investigation to show they were real. In the same issue, *True* magazine quoted an anonymous USAF spokesman who said: 'We don't know what these things were and there's no use pretending we do.'

While the USAF and its investigators were stumped, the US government knew just what to do. Within months of the Washington sightings, the CIA convened the Robertson Panel, which recommended using all means available to allay any public interest in the UFO phenomenon – and the cover-up and the debunking started.

The cover-up continues to this day and it involves not just the US military, but also the military authorities of America's European allies. In the summer of 1998, a four-day workshop reviewed all the physical evidence associated with UFO sightings across Europe that had been accumulated by seven top UFO researchers. They paid particular attention to radar contacts. This presented difficulties, as the workshop's report states: 'The panel concludes from these presentations that the analysis of radar records is a very specialised activity that requires the services of radar experts. The panel also notes that information from military radar can be obtained only with the co-operation of military authorities, and that most military authorities do not offer this co-operation... further study of this phenomenon by means of radar-visual cases may not be feasible unless the relevant authorities recognise the mission of an official UFO research organisation.'

Pacific panic

In the months after the Japanese attack on Pearl Harbor, America was on tenterhooks. An attack on the mainland, perhaps a full-scale invasion, was expected at any time. On the evening of 25 February 1942, air observers reported aircraft approaching the Pacific coast near Los Angeles. At around 7:20 p.m., lights were seen in the sky near an important defence plant. At 2 a.m., radar reported unidentified contacts out over the sea. Air-raid sirens sounded. Los Angeles was plunged into darkness and anti-aircraft guns filled the skies with flack. A formation of UFOs flew over the city, high and very fast. The guns continued pounding for another hour. When they eventually fell silent, it was found that the city had not been attacked. No bombs had been dropped. No aircraft downed. The only damage done to the city was caused by anti-aircraft shells.

Canadian Contacts

In the later 1940s and early 1950s Goose Bay in Labrador became a UFO hotspot. On 29 October 1948 a UFO was tracked by radar as it streaked across the bay. The following night it returned. This time contact was maintained for four minutes and it was calculated that the object was travelling at over 625 miles an hour.

Two years later, a UFO was seen in the same area by Captain James Howard, a pilot with BOAC. On closer examination, he saw that it was actually a mothership accompanied by a gaggle of other flying objects. They fled when he approached. The sighting received huge press coverage and even prompted Air Chief Marshall Lord Dowding to say that he believed in flying saucers.

The UFO returned to Goose Bay on 19 June 1952, when a strange red light appeared in the sky over Goose Bay Air Base. It was also picked up by radar. Witnesses on the ground saw the light suddenly turn white and increase in brilliance. At the same time, the radar contact seemed to flare. Then it disappeared simultaneously from sight and the radar screen.

Visual Confirmation

On the night of 13 August 1956, multiple radar contacts were made over RAF Bentwaters in Suffolk. Six ground stations and one airborne station independently reported five contacts with objects flying at incredible speeds. Twenty radar personnel confirmed the contacts. Nine visual observers confirmed the contacts with sightings of brilliantly lit objects in the sky.

The first contact was made by Bentwaters Ground Control Approach Radar, which calculated that the object was travelling at speed of around 4,250 miles an hour. Other slower objects followed in its wake. Bentwaters asked for confirmation from the USAF base at RAF Lakenheath. When it was received, the RAF scrambled two fighters to investigate the intruders. One of them was vectored on an intercept course. It had both visual and radar contact. But suddenly the ground station saw the UFO double back and begin to chase the fighter. The pursuit continued for several minutes before the UFO disappeared. The pilot returned home safely, though shaken and puzzled.

The Guardian

UFOs returned to Canada in 1989. An object was tracked on radar before it fell towards the ground near West Carleton, to the west of Ottawa, on 4 November. The area was immediately sealed off and huge helicopters and military units, specially trained to deal with UFO retrievals, were flown in. The source of this story, who called himself the 'Guardian', also said that the aliens themselves were tracked on radar.

The Guardian said that the alien craft used a pulsing electromagnetic field to fly and was built from a matrixed-dielectric magnesium alloy. It also generated cold fusion radiation. He also said that the alien mission had a malevolent purpose. It was the start of an alien invasion.

MUFON's Bob Oeschler, a former NASA mission specialist, investigated. The Guardian sent him a package in February 1992. The package contained a video, several documents and maps of the area. The tape was thirty minutes long, with the first six minutes showing actual movement, the rest was just stills. The video showed strange lights, movements of 'aliens' around the craft and also a full-frontal shot of an alien's face.

The video was analysed and it had signs of editing, also the scenes of the craft were duplicated by researchers using toy remote controlled helicopters, some flashing lights and some flares. They were also able to purchase an alien mask from a costume shop identical to the one in the video. This case eventually caused Oeschler to resign from MUFON.

Physical Evidence

Not all UFO encounters depend for their credibility on the relia-
bilty of eyewitnesses, photographs that can be faked or radar contacts that can be withheld by the authorities. Sometimes alien craft
leave physical evidence.

One of these cases occurred in the small agricultural settlement
of Delphos, Texas. One November evening in 1971, sixteen-year-
old farm hand Ronnie Johnson was just finishing his day's work
when he suddenly looked up to see a large, mushroom-shaped
UFO, hovering just above the ground in front of him. Caught
unawares, he was paralysed with fear and the light from the craft
was so bright it temporarily blinded him. After a few moments, the
craft began to ascend and Ronnie came to his senses and ran off to
get his parents. He returned with them in time to see the UFO
shooting rapidly up into the sky. But had that been the end of the
story, it is unlikely that anyone would have believed them.

However, on the ground in front of them, in the very place the
object had been hovering, they saw a circle in the earth about eight
feet across that was glowing brightly. It did not appear to be hot and
Ronnie's mother bent down and touched the glowing ring. As she
did so, her fingers became frozen and numb. They remained that
way for several weeks after the encounter.

This case became one of the most thoroughly investigated in the
history UFOlogy. But it was far from unique. Thousands of UFO
encounters have left behind physical evidence. Investigators call
them 'physical trace cases', or encounters of the second kind. They
provide the most solid evidence alien spacecraft have visited Earth.

The world's leading expert on physical trace cases, Ted Phillips,
investigated the Delphos case. A civil engineer from Branson,
Missouri, Phillips has visited four hundred and fifty UFO sites and
investigated some six hundred encounters over the past thirty
years. From his studies, he says that around the world over five
thousand UFO trace cases have been reported.

Phillips first became interested in UFOs when his father told
him about a pilot who had been buzzed by a flying saucer. He
began to investigate sightings in his home state of Missouri in the

1960s. In 1966, he came across a case in Florida where contactee John Reeves had photographed the footprint of an alien after one had visited his home.

The first case that brought Phillips to prominence occurred the following year. Three men were out hunting when they saw a fly-ing saucer descend into the valley where they had been camping. No only did the men manage to photograph the UFO, they also had physical evidence of it. It swooped so low that it had scorched a tree and damaged the men's camping equipment. Phillips docu-mented the case and took his findings to established UFO researcher Dr J. Allen Hynek of North Western University. Hynek, who is often described as the 'father of UFOlogy', was so impressed that he asked Phillips to work out a methodology for the systematic investigation of physical trace cases. They worked together until Hynek's death in 1986.

According to Phillips' definition, a physical trace case is a UFO sighting where one or more people witness an object, on or near the ground, and once the object leaves the area a number of physical changes to the environment can be found. In the cases Phillips has investigated, these have included impressions left in the ground from landing gear, rings of crushed vegetation and burnt soil, and even alien footprints. He has also come across a number of hoaxes.

'They were very easy to spot,' he says. 'People pour petrol on the ground, ignite it and try to make a ring. Sometimes they simply dig indentations in the soil, but when you've seen hundreds of examples of real traces caused by a UFO, you realise that the effects are very specific and extremely difficult to replicate.'

When he arrives at the sight of a UFO encounter, the first thing Phillips does look for signs of a possible hoax. But at Delphos he was soon satisfied that the case is genuine and began taking soil samples with a cylindrical boring inside and outside the ring. Chemical analysis revealed that the soil from inside the ring had been completely dehydrated down to a depth of fourteen inches. The soil would not even rehydrate when placed in water. But when soil from outside the ring was put in water, it dissolved readily.

The soil in the ring remained affected for quite some time. Six months later, the area was covered by a heavy show fall. When Phillips cleared off the snow and threw a bucket of water on to the soil, the ring reappeared, as the soil there still refused to absorb water.

Phillips carries out most of his work without using professional laboratories. This cuts out the cost of expensive lab work, but Phillips is also suspicious of labs that are directly connected to the government. He believes that they could not be relied upon if his evidence was about to yield significant findings.

'Given the fact that the government is obviously covering up a great deal of information regarding the UFO phenomenon,' Phillips says, 'it would be overly optimistic to think they would help provide evidence for the existence of visiting UFOs.'

But Phillips made an exception in the Delphos case, because there was no other way to find out why soil was so determinedly dehydrated. Phillips called in the help of the leading UFOlogist Stanton Friedman. They had worked together on a number of UFO cases. Friedman found an independent lab called Agra-Science, which specialised in doing soil analysis for farmers. The lab tested Phillip's soil samples for thermo-luminescence to reveal whether the earth had been subjected to intense heat. According to Friedman, the results showed that the soil had been irradiated by some intense form of energy, possibly microwaves.

The soil samples were also sent to another independent laboratory at Oak Ridge. The scientists there examined them under an electron microscope and discovered that the soil had strange crystalline structures, unlike anything they had even seen before. The soil particles were coated in a mysterious substance, which explained why they could not absorb water.

Phillips tried growing seeds in the affected soil, using soil taken from outside the ring as a control. The seeds would not germinate in the affected soil, though they flourished in the control. Eventually, though, the soil recovered and plants began to grow in it again.

Categories of Evidence

The Delphos case is only one of hundreds of UFO cases where physical traces have been left that have been investigated by Ted Phillips. Phillips has assembled a huge amount of evidence. He has been able to divide physical trace cases into three broad categories. One involves the classic disc-shaped flying saucer, metallic in appearance and thirty to forty feet in diameter. When they land, witnesses often seen humanoid aliens in the area. These flying saucers leave a scorched ring of soil about thirty feet in diameter and indentations thought to be left by the landing gear.

Then there are small circular objects, eight to ten feet in diameter, which often glow brightly. They leave a smaller ring of singed or dehydrated soil. A scorched earth ring of this sort was found in Kofu City, Japan, in 1975, when Masato Kohno saw a UFO land.

Egg-shaped craft leave four indentations, again thought to be made by landing gear. From Phillips' tests of the soil compression in these marks, they would have to be made by an object weighing some twenty-five tonnes.

Phillips has also investigated so-called 'saucer nests'. These are circular areas of flattened crops that appear in fields. They show none of the intricate patterns of crop circles and often show genetic mutations in the plants not normally associated with crop circles. As Phillips' trace cases always involve sightings, he distinguishes 'saucer nest' cases from crop circles – which do not – and believes that they may be two separate phenomena. Similar 'saucer nests' appeared in France in 1990.

Footprints

Some 23 per cent of physical trace cases involve the sighting of the craft's alien occupants and sometimes Phillips is lucky enough to get a photograph or a plaster cast of an alien footprint.

'If we get word of the landing a week or a month after it happened, the chances are that the site would be so beaten down by the weather or local people that any footprints would have been destroyed,' he says. 'In cases where the information has reached us earlier, we have found either a partial footprint or a series of fresh ones.'

He frequently runs into footprints of Greys, who leave footprints like an impression from a moccasin, the size and depth of those left by a small child.

Phillips' work has been officially dismissed and derided. But Friedman maintains that the evidence he presents is indisputable.

'What we are looking at here is empirical evidence that just cannot be dismissed by the "noisy negativists",' he says. 'Hallucinations cannot dehydrate fourteen inches of soil. Nor consistently leave physical, testable and tangible evidence such as phosphorescent rings in the earth.'

Beach Bummer

A UFO crashed on the beach at Ubatuba, Brazil in September 1957. Ibrahim Sued, a journalist with leading Brazilian newspaper *O Globo*, received a letter about it on 13 September. The letter was signed and read:

'As a faithful reader of your column and your admirer, I wish to give you something of the highest interest to a newspaper man, about the flying discs. If you believe that they are real, of course. I didn't believe anything said or published about them. But just a few days ago I was forced to change my mind. I was fishing together with some friends, at a place close to the town of Ubatuba, Sao Paulo, when I sighted a flying disc. It approached the beach at an

Examining a presumed UFO landing site, near Richmond, Virginia, USA

Tully, Queensland, Australia, 1966: area of flattened reeds, possibly made by UFO.

unbelievable speed and an accident – a crash into the sea – seemed imminent. At the last moment, however, when it was almost striking the waters, it made a sharp turn upward and climbed rapidly on a fantastic impulse. We followed the spectacle with our eyes, startled, when we saw the disk explode in flames. It disintegrated into thousands of fiery fragments, which fell sparkling with magnificent brightness. They looked like fireworks, despite the time of the accident, which was noon. Most of these fragments, almost all, fell into the sea. But a number of small pieces fell close to the beach and we picked up a large amount of this material, which was as light as paper. I am enclosing a small sample of it. I don't know anyone that could be trusted to whom I might send it for analysis. I never read about a flying disc being found, or about fragments or parts of a saucer that had been picked up.'

Sued sent two of the three samples to the Aerial Phenomena Research Organisation, a UFO group in Tucson Arizona, while the third was retained by Brazilian UFOlogist Dr Olavo Fontes for further study.

The three samples looked like pieces of irregular and highly oxidised metal, coloured dull whitish grey. Dr Fontes' sample was

Martians' footprints in the sand, after a UFO landing at the home of John Reeves, Florida, USA. in December 1966.

tested at the mineral production labs in the Brazilian agricultural ministry. They applied chemical, spectrographic analysis and X-ray diffusion techniques on the metal. These tests indicated that the material was very pure magnesium. The chemist also noted that the normal trace elements expected in magnesium samples were all missing.

Fontes used up all of his sample in a series of further tests. Part of it went to a chemist who conducted an X-ray investigation at the labs of a geology unit. The geology lab determined that the magnesium was of a very high purity, with a reading of 1.87, compared with a normal reading of 1.74. Pieces were also sent to the Brazilian Army and Navy research departments, but both the Army and Navy kept their findings secret.

ARPO sent a sample to the USAF, but the sample they sent met with an 'accident' while they were testing it. The USAF asked for a further sample to be sent. APRO declined. They tried to conduct tests with remaining the sample but it soon became too small to be of any use. APRO still retains one small chunk in their vaults.

Alien Artefacts

Those who have had contact with aliens have often tried to bring back some sort of alien artefact with them as proof of their contact. Betty Hill asked the aliens who abducted her whether she could take one of their books. At first, they seemed to give their permission, then changed their mind. Maybe the aliens have got wary because evidence they have supplied before has been comprehensively derided.

Howard Menger, one of the first alien contactees in the 1950s, was taken to the Moon and brought back a lunar potato. It was sent to the analysts LaWall-Harrisson Consultants in Philadelphia. They found that potato was indistinguishable from the terrestrial variety, however the protein content was some five times higher than that of any Earth potato. At that time, the UFO community was still very trusting and no one suspected that the government was conducting a cover-up, secretly exploiting alien technology for their own ends, or that the military and intelligence agencies were colluding with the aliens. So Menger naively sent his extraterrestrial spud to the Central Intelligence Agency. The CIA jumped at the chance of analysing the specimen. Two weeks later, Menger and his wife visited the CIA laboratories and were allowed to watch the analysis in progress. They were shown pieces of potato under the microscope and other pieces soaking in various fluids in sample jars. Menger was impressed with the rigour of their approach. He never heard from them again.

Alien Implants

Since the Earth was first visited by flying saucers, there have been some people who have doubted the existence of our extraterrestrial visitors. These sceptics have found the idea of alien abduction even harder to swallow. But fortunately, many abductees can prove what they have been saying. They have physical proof in the form of alien implants.

Like many abductees, Pat Parrinello experienced strange phenomena from childhood. It began when he was just six; he was woken by a brilliant light in his bedroom and found himself paralysed. Since then he has had many such experiences. He has been monitored constantly by aliens and visited by the familiar, large-headed Greys.

Unlike most alien abductees, Parrinello has full conscious recall of his experiences and has not had to resort to regressional hypnosis. He clearly remembers every detail of the abduction, including the humiliating medical examinations that most people manage to blank out.

It was after one abduction that Parrinello was convinced that aliens implanted a small device in his hand. It showed up clearly on an X-ray. And in August 1995, he became one of the first abductees to undergo surgery to retrieve an alien implant. This was no simple matter. After Parrinello took the decision to have the implant removed, he suffered weeks of alien intervention designed to stop him. He suffered severe head pains and often found the abductors' UFO following him. Nevertheless he was determined to go ahead.

The operation was done by Dr Roger Leir in his offices in Ventura, California. Parrinello had been taken to Leir by UFOlogist Derrel Sims, who was investigating the case. At the same time Sims was also investigating the abduction case of a woman named Janet, who had an implant in her foot. Leir operated on her at the same time.

The operations had to be carried out under conditions of the strictest security. Dr Leir was afraid that he might risk losing his licence for performing such an unconventional procedure.

'People with credibility who put themselves forward in this field can wind up out of business,' said Leir

Nevertheless Leir risked having the entire procedure videoed. Although the tapes could have been used against him in any medical ethics hearing, he knew they would be vital in establishing the validity of what he was doing.

Leir began the operations with an experiment. With the patient under a strong local anaesthetic, which numbed all sensation in the area of the implant, Leir tapped the implant gently. Both Parrinello and Janet jerked violently in response. It was all Leir could do to prevent Janet leaping from the operating table. There was no doubt that the anaesthetic was working and Dr Leir had no explanation for their reactions.

Next Leir used a meter to detect any magnetic field given off by the implants. It showed a massive reaction. The needle practically went off the scale, indicating a powerful electromagnetic field. This made removing the implant difficult using surgical implements with metal blades. But when the implants were removed the field miraculously dissipated.

An object 4 mm by 2 mm was retrieved from Parrinello's hand. It was dark and covered in a membrane made of keratin and haemoglobin. These are both proteins found naturally in the body. This casing was the sort of covering that builds up around all foreign matter that enters the body and its genetic fingerprint showed a DNA match with Parrinello. But Leir was certain that it was not a cyst or anything else that grew naturally in the body. He had seen nothing like it before. It was so strong that it could not be cut open by a sharp surgical scalpel. It also contained numerous nerve endings. This may explained the Parrinello's response when it was tapped.

'If these objects were actually left in the body by alien beings, it would not be difficult for the aliens to adapt them by forming them along the lines of the body's own chemistry,' says abduction expert Professor Mack.

Leir had to make a deep incision to remove two objects from Janet's toe. They were of similar composition, were triangular in shape and measured 1.5 mm by 1.5 mm. Sims sent all three to the University of Houston for more detailed investigation. Scientists there discovered that,

Alleged alien implant found in roof of an abductee's mouth.

under the organic membrane, they were made of shiny, black metal strips. Chemical analysis indicated that the implants are metallic and consisted of eleven different elements, including boron, a metalloid substance used to harden steel, which does not occur naturally in the body.

It was also discovered that the implants glowed green when subjected to ultra-violet light. Sims used this property to detect implants under the skin of other abductees. This led to the recovery of another thirteen alien implants from the bodies of abductees in 1996. Sims has collected more than thirty in all.

Despite this concrete evidence, some sceptics are still not convinced. Arch-debunker Philip Klass claims that there is no provable link between the alien implants and extraterrestrials. Although abductees believe that the implants are used by the aliens to monitor them, Klass says that the devices have no obvious purpose and claims that they are mundane growths that can exist inside the body for years without the host noticing because they cause no discomfort or pain. Klass points out that Parrinello had a swelling in the region of the hand where the implant was found as long ago as 1984. However, just because the implant has been in his body for a long time does not mean that it is terrestrial.

What exactly the implants are for, even Sims admits, no one knows. But they had been surgically implanted in people who had no record of surgery, so they must have some purpose, he reasons. Some researchers believe that they are tracking devices – like the transponders not much bigger than a grain of rice programmed with an electronic code that ostrich farmers implant in the neck of their birds to keep track of them. However, Sims does not believe they are tracking devices. He thinks that they are some sort of monitoring device, although they may also be used to control abductees.

Implant Programme

There is a discernible implant programme underway. The earliest reported abduction case occurred in late 1957. No implants were associated with abductions for nearly ten years. Then in 1966, scars began appearing on the bodies of abductees, though they were not recognised in any numbers until the mid-1970s. The vast majority of implant cases seem to have occurred in the US, critics say, pointing out that scars are rarer in abductees in other countries, even where abductions are numerous. However, this is probably because more of an effort is made to look for them in America.

But implants are not unknown in other countries. Social worker and UFOlogist Keith Basterfield investigated the case of 'Susan', a young abductee from Adelaide, South Australia. She had her first contact with aliens when she was ten years old in 1971. Two different species of aliens were involved in Susan's abduction. Tall humanoids were in command, while the small, large headed Greys did all the menial jobs.

A number of encounters ensued over the years. These involved periodical medical examinations to monitor her development. Then in 1991, during a routine visit to the dentist, an X-ray was taken. This showed a shadowy, unidentified object implanted in her mouth. To investigate this, a second X-ray was arranged for a few weeks later. But in the mean time, Susan was abducted again and the implant removed. The second X-ray showed no trace, and meanwhile the first set of X-rays had gone missing.

Surveys have suggested that as many as one in three people can find an unusual scar of unknown origin on their body, if they looked for one. This could mean that a third of the population has been abducted at one time or another. Abductees believed implants were first placed in their bodies in the late 1970s. Most said the devices were being implanted by forcing them up the nose. Abductees often wake from their abduction with a severe nosebleed.

The number of implantation cases rose meteorically in the 1980s. By the end of the decade, about one in four abductees had implants. The aliens had broadened their scope and were implanting in the head, via the mouth and the ear as well as the nose. Then in the 1990s, implants were discovered in other parts of the body, such as the foot and the hand – as in the cases investigated by Sims and removed by Leir in 1995. But these cases are still uncommon.

Implant Investigation

The most extensive scientific examination of an alien implant was undertaken by Dr David Pritchard, a physicist from the Massachusetts Institute of Technology. He undertook a full study of an implant recovered from the genitals of a male host, who believes that he was first abducted from his home in New York in 1955. Despite examining the object under an electron microscope and subjecting it to the very latest techniques of mass spectroscopy, he was unable to identify it – although this does not actually prove that it was of alien origin.

'Analysis shows nothing "unterrestrial" about it, quite the opposite,' he says. 'It does not appear to be fabricated, but rather has the overall characteristics of something that grew. [But] it is possible that the aliens are so clever that they can make devices to serve their purposes yet [which] appear to have a prosaic origin as natural products of the human body.'

But American researcher Martin Cannon has a more sinister explanation. He believes that abductees are not being kidnapped by aliens at all, but by some covert arm of the US government, possibly the CIA. The implants are mind control devices that makes ordinary members of the public the unwilling and unconscious slave of the intelligence community. The abduction memories are planted deep in their minds by post-hypnotic suggestion – that's why they usually have to be retrieved by hypnotic regression. The memories of the alien abduction cloak any memory of what really happened. Even if the screen slips and the abductee remembers what really happened, they are easily discredited because they have already claimed that they were abducted by aliens and – in the public's eyes – are already seen as 'kinda flaky'.

Crop Circles

Early one morning in July 1991, Rita Goold got lucky. She and her fellow crop circle investigators were holding vigil near the tiny Wiltshire hamlet of Alton Barnes, where on previous occasions some of the most celebrated crop circles had made an appearance. Shortly after 3 a.m., as the dawn mist crept across the field, a luminous white tube descended from a cloud, slowly at first, pouring forth what the witnesses described as a fluid-like substance. Narrowly missing the field, it hit the ground on a nearby hill.

'As it came down', said Goold, 'it shot out two arms, covering the top of the hill – it must have been eight hundred feet across – and in each arm all this stuff was pouring in, finding rivulets, clouding and making formations, and as it was doing this, the tube was emptying. Then the tube collapsed and vanished.'

The event lasted eight seconds in all.

'It was like something out of a Steven Spielberg movie,' Goold said. Another colleague described it as 'biblical'.

The next day Goold and her friends could find no trace of any disturbance when they visited the hillside in daylight. However, news spread through the crop circle fraternity that Goold and her mates discovered the mechanism behind the crop circle phenomenon.

Dr Terence Meaden was particularly thrilled. He had spent years investigating the phenomenon. But while many insisted that crop circles were caused by flying saucers coming into land, Meaden had consistently argued that there must be a purely scientific explanation.

Meaden had studied tornadoes and put forward the hypothesis that a static vortex of ionised air – similar to a tornado – was responsible for even the most complex patterns. He called the mechanism responsible a 'plasma vortex'. It was, he maintained, a rare but entirely natural effect that occurred only in certain climatic and topographical conditions.

Although crop circles appeared to be a relatively a recent phenomenon, Meaden believed that crop circles had once provided the inspiration for prehistoric stone circles in the area. He also said that his plasma vortices might explain UFO sightings. Blasphemy indeed.

On the other side of the fence, there were those who said that, although the first crude crop circles were caused by UFOs landing, their alien occupants had discovered that they were a good way to announce their presence to humankind. After all, the complex

Crop circles at Westbury, Wiltshire, 1988.

patterns they were producing showed all the hallmarks of intelligent design. A third faction agreed that non-human intelligence was involved, but pointed the finger at Gaia – the notion that the Earth itself is an intelligent entity – or other paranormal entities or psychic energies. To Meaden and his supporters, these theories came from the crankier end of New Age beliefs. But certainly something extraordinary was going on. The pilot of a light aircraft saw an eighty to ninety foot circle formation in a field near Stonehenge, which must have been created in just 45 minutes. It followed the Fibonacci series, forming a highly complex pattern seen in fractal geometry. It had not been there when he flew over the same field three-quarters of an hour earlier.

'At every stage, the circles phenomenon stretches and tests our perception of reality,' said one researcher.

Snowflake patters, spider's webs and the double helix of DNA appeared, along with alien circuit diagrams and star maps, and geometric designs where the flattered crops were brushed in various directions, simulating texture.

'Whatever, or whoever, made them is an artist of genius,' said John McEwen, art critic of the *Sunday Times*. Others compared them to modern-day devotional art that uses mystical symbols and sacred geometry to communicate with the world beyond. Or perhaps it was the world beyond using mystical symbols and sacred geometry to communicate with us.

'This force may be powerful enough to act as a catalyst for the many physiological and psychological effects – both curative and malevolent – that are often attributed to circles,' said investigator Rob Irving.

The Men Who Fooled the World

As the design of the circles became more and more complex, Dr Meaden found it increasingly difficult to explain them using his plasma vortex theory and, privately, he began to suspect there was a simpler explanation. There was. Their names were Doug Bower and Dave Chorley. These two Southampton-based sexagenarians – known as Doug and Dave in the tabloids – claimed to be 'The Men Who Fooled the World'. For fifteen years they had been sneaking into the fields of Hampshire and south Wiltshire and creating complex crop circles with nothing more than a three-foot wooden board and some string. They had all winter to plan the next year's circles and, each summer, they were determined to outdo the previous year's designs. They both had a keen interest in art and sought out inspiration in galleries and libraries. The first design for one of their early efforts – two circles joined by an avenue and flanked by sets of short, parallel bars – was pinched from a book on Russian painting.

Although they were denied recognition, they enjoyed the fact that their creations were being hailed as the work of a higher intelligence. But they got a bit peeved when researchers began publishing books and making money out of their latest alien entity theory. So they decided to reveal all and went to the newspapers, only to discover that few committed researchers accepted their story.

Journalists soon unearthed other groups of covert circle makers. The artist Rod Dickenson also admitted that he had made circles.

Crop circles: 'pictogram' formation at Alton Barnes, Wiltshire, July 1990.

Crop circles, southern England, 1996: Windmill Hill, Avebury, Wiltshire.

They used tape measures, balls of string, garden rollers and specially constructed devices made out of pram wheels to flatten the crops. 'I make art for people who don't realise it's art,' he explained. 'What is really an art experience is interpreted as a paranormal experience.' Some journalists also admitted making circles during their investigations of hoaxing, further perpetuating phenomenon. *The Guardian* even sponsored a circle hoaxing competition in 1992, which was won by a team from Westland Helicopters who called themselves 'Masters of the Cereal Universe'.

Were the Hoaxers a Hoax?

While Dr Terence Meaden and his scientific colleagues were happy to cede the field, those who believed in an extraterrestrial author were not. Rumours spread that Doug and Dave – along with anyone else who supported the hoax theory – were merely pawns in a much deeper conspiracy to discredit the circles. And who was behind this conspiracy? Whitehall, the CIA and extreme factions of the church were blamed. Even such distinguished UFOlogists as Jacques Vallee talked of crop circles being caused by the testing of top-secret space-weapons, spun off from the 'Star Wars' programme. The human circle makers were simply being used to muddy the water for serious researchers.

Some more benign souls wondered what mysterious forces inspired Doug and Dave.

'Many human circle makers are, after all, reluctant to claim individual formations as their own work,' said the ever optimistic Rob Irving. 'Perhaps they are aware of a greater force at work, an inherently mysterious guiding hand which shapes and controls their nocturnal efforts.'

By the summer of 1993, the anti-hoax faction knew that they needed hard evidence to support their position. They began applying the strictest scientific methods to their work. They took soil samples and samples of the crops themselves and tested them for evidence of microwave radiation, or intense heat. Some researchers detected changes in the plants' crystalline structures. Others showed differences in the growth rates between seeds taken from the plants flattened in the circles and those taken from the standing crops around them. A wealthy American research team found, in one large formation, minute emissions from radioactive isotopes that do not occur naturally. However, the sceptics were happy to stick with Doug and Dave's story.

The litmus test was to find a way to tell a hoaxed circle from a genuine one. The man who applied his mind to this task was a Michigan-based biophysicist, Dr William C. Levengood. His analysis confirmed that samples displayed anomalous variations. They showed significant differences in their cellular structures when compared to control samples. Both abnormally high and low radiation levels were both found. Most significantly, he found that samples of wheat and the local chalk were covered in a rust-coloured, glaze-like substance he discovered to be meteoric dust. On the other hand, as a scientist, he did not entirely dismiss Terry Meade's work. His conclusion was that crop circles were made by intelligently controlled plasma vortices.

Scientific Encounters

Close Encounters Classified

Things used to be so easy. In olden days, when someone saw a strange phenomenon in the sky, it was an angel or a fiery chariot or a pillar of light or glowing crucifixes. But with the advent of the UFO in the second half of the twentieth century things got altogether more problematic.

For sceptics though, things are still easy. UFO reports fall into just two categories: the misidentifications of a mundane object or the result of some mental aberration. But the fledgling science of UFOlogy began to look for ways to classify real physical flying objects. To quantify and qualify accounts of UFO encounters and to give the subject the gloss of scientific empiricism, UFOlogists began to categorise reports based on the shape of the object, its movement and the witnesses' level of interaction with it. The idea was to find a way to analyse the UFO data statistically and work out whether there were any patterns underlying it.

To start with there was very little interaction between human witness and the craft they saw, but as UFO sighting reports and photographs flooded in, in the wake of Kenneth Arnold's saucer sighting of 1947, 'saucerology' concentrated its attention on what the flying craft looked like and it was discovered that they came in seven essential varieties:

1. **Disc-shaped** – These are the classic flying saucer, flat and round like an ice-hockey puck. Most have a domed upper section, making them more like a hub cap. Some are domed on both the upper and lower surfaces, and some have a broad rim. Disc-shaped UFOs include the flying saucers seen by Kenneth Arnold, the probe ships photographed by Paul Villa, the craft that took George Adamski to the Moon and the 'sports model' that Bob Lazar worked on in Area 51. The most famous photograph of a disc-shaped UFO was taken by Paul Trent over his farm in Oregon in 1950.

2. **Spheroid** – These are globe-shaped craft, although they also
    appear as elongated or flattened spheres, as ovoid or egg-
    shaped or as SLOs – Saturn-like objects that are spheroid with
    a band around the middle. These were particular common in
    Europe from medieval times and appear in woodcarvings – a
    fine example comes from Basel, Switzerland in 1566. Almira
    Baruana photographed an SLO over Trindad in 1958, and
    Robert Taylor had an encounter with an ovoid craft about
    twenty feet across in a forest clearing in Scotland in 1979. Two
    round objects with spikes knocked him to the ground. When he
    regained consciousness, all three were gone.

UFOs photographed over Conisbrough, South Yorkshire, by Stephen Pratt,

UFOs over Italy, 26
September 1960.

3. **Cylinder** – These cigar-shaped objects are almost as common
as saucer-shaped craft and may explain the phantom airships
that were seen at the end of the nineteenth century. One of the
earliest sightings of this type of craft in modern times was
made by Ella Fortune, a nurse from the Mescalero Indian
Reservation in New Mexico, on 16 October 1957. She saw it

UFO ('luminous disc') photographed over Paris, France, 29 December 1953 by
engineer Paul Paulin. 2-minute exposure, during which the motionless UFO
jumped sideways and again remained motionless.

hovering over nearby Holloman Air Force Base. Like discs, these craft sometimes have domed protuberances, tapered or rounded ends, portholes or fins. They are not as common as they used to be. The most famous example is George Adamski's 'mothership', for which he provided detailed specifications.

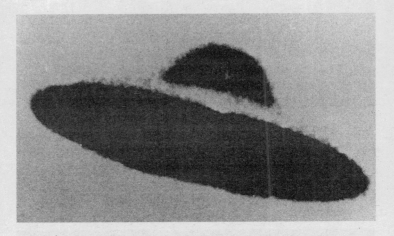

Close-up of UFO photographed by George J. Stock at Passic, New Jersey,

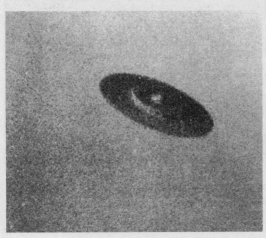

UFO at Barra da Tijuca, Brazil, 7 May 1952.

American military plane, S-47, saw dark red UFO at 400 metres over Utah, 1966, and pilot took this photograph

During aerial photography mission over Costa Rica in 1971, a UFO appeared on one frame of the film. Previous and following frames were clear - they were taken at 17-second intervals.

UFO photographed 12 March 1967 by New Mexico State University student west of Picacho Peak, New Mexico, USA.

UFO photographed by contactee Harold Trudel, in East Woonsocket, Rhode Island, USA, 10 June 1967.

UFO photographed 3 July 1960 between Cordoba and Yacanto, Argentina, by Captain Hugo Niotti of the Argentine Air Force (later Vice Commodore).

4.   **Flying Triangles** – These triangular-shaped craft have become
common since the late 1980s. There is some argument whether
they are extraterrestrial craft at all. They are possibly man-
made as part of black projects that back-engineer technology
from downed alien craft. They are commonly seen at night and
are identified by the triangular arrangement of the lights on the
underside. They vary in size enormously, from relatively small
craft to ones half-a-mile across. They vary in shape, too. Some
are conical, like the one Ron and Paula Watson of Mount
Vernon, Missouri, saw in 1983, when its occupants were muti-
lating one of their cows. David Spoor of Norfolk photographed some smaller, more agile triangles in 1998.

5.   **Polygonal** – These are craft with more than three sides, such
as the diamond-shaped craft that abducted Betty Cash and
Vicki Landrum in December 1980 or the five-pointed star seen
over Australia the same day in 1978 that Frederick Valentich
disappeared. A pentagonal UFO hovered over Shiogama City
in Japan in September 1986. It was seen by more than twenty
people and photographed by Akira Maezuka.

6.   **Balls of light** – These are among the most common UFOs
sighted. They occur as a single point of light, but more often
come in formations. The most famous example is the 'string of
pearls' photographed by student Carl Hart over Lubbock,
Texas in 1952. They are often dismissed as a natural phenomenon, such as bolides or 'earthlights' – coloured lights thought
to be produced over areas of tectonic stress – and are often
seen at Hessdalen, Norway, or over the Yakima Indian
Reservation in Washington State. However, the witnesses
often report that the unidentified lights are attached to or sur-
round a solid craft.

7.   **Exotic** – This is the category where sightings of UFOs that do
not fit into any of the other categories end up. They are usually one-offs. In 1967 RAF Intelligence Officer J.B.W. 'Angus'

Brooks saw a huge flying object that took the form of a giant cross. In 1996, a number of witnesses saw a 150-foot high rotating octagonal pyramid over Pelatos, Brazil. One witness, Haroldo Westendorff, was flying his light aircraft when he encountered it. He said that he saw its peak open and a disc-shaped object fly out. The sighting was confirmed by local air traffic controllers. A seventy-one-year-old Polish farmer named Jan Wolski saw a barn-shaped flying object. A family who also saw it said it had multicoloured rotating corkscrews coming out of the corners. And hundreds of witnesses saw a huge boomerang-shape fly over the West Coast.

The first truly scientific attempt at classifying UFOs came from the most influential figure in early UFOlogy, Dr. Josef Allen Hynek. A professor of astronomy at Northwestern University, Hynek was employed in 1948 by the US Air Force to investigate UFO reports. He was consultant to the three major Air Force UFO studies – Projects Sign, Grudge and Blue Book. Although these programmes were largely designed to debunk UFO sightings, Hynek became convinced that there was a real mystery at the heart of the UFO phenomenon. So, after Blue Book was closed, he established the Center for UFO Studies (CUFOS), which remains one of the largest UFO groups in the world, to continue his research.

Hynek's most famous contribution to UFOlogy was his famous 'close encounter' classification system, which was brought to public attention by the Steven Spielberg movie *Close Encounters of the Third Kind* in 1977. Spielberg gave Hynek a walk-on part in the film in recognition of his contribution. Hynek's classification system lent some much-needed scientific weight to the otherwise outlandish UFO reports.

Hynek gave UFOlogy intellectual respectability by recognising that sighting reports were its principal source of data. Rather than dismissing reports because they seemed bizarre, Hynek insisted that witnesses should be listened to. Their reports were real evidence that required proper scientific evaluation. Hynek divided accounts into two types: those where the witness was more than five hundred feet from the object and those where the witness was less than five hundred feet from the object – so-called close encounters.

Within the first category, he identified three different types of report. These were:

1. **Nocturnal lights** – These are lights in the sky that cannot be accounted for by man-made craft, meteorological or astronomical phenomena.

2. **Daylight discs** – These are solid craft, not necessarily disc-shaped, that cannot be accounted for by man-made craft.

3. **Radar visual** – These are anomalous readings on an electronic device, not necessarily radar, that cannot be explained by any man-made phenomena.

The second category – the close encounters – was also subdivided into three types:

1. **Close encounters of the first kind (CEI)** – This is where the witness comes within five hundred feet of an anomalous object, but it has no interaction with the witness or the environment.

2. **Close encounters of the second kind (CEII)** – This is where the witness comes within five hundred feet of an anomalous object that leaves some damage or physical evidence in the environment.

3. **Close encounters of the third kind (CEIII)** – This is where alien beings are seen inside or close to the object, and who may or may not have some contact with the witness.

Since Hynek first devised this system, the relationship between humankind and aliens has moved on apace, and it has been necessary to add new categories. There are now close encounters of the fourth kind (CEIV). These occur when witnesses experience mental or physical changes due to direct interaction with alien beings. Close encounters of the fifth kind (CEV) involve witnesses who can initiate encounters by contacting aliens physically or mentally. Then there are close encounters of the sixth kind (CEVI), where the witness is 'possessed' by a non-physical alien entity.

Hynek did not include these last three categories in his system because he was sceptical about abduction accounts. He did not feel that there was enough solid evidence in abduction reports to evaluate them scientifically. However, since he died in 1986, a new generation of UFOlogists has made full use of these new classifications.

Although Hynek's system is still the most widely used system of classification, many UFOlogists feel that it is too crude to be useful in investigating modern encounters. Some have tried to devise other systems, but these attempts have usually come to grief. Either they are overly complicated or they rely too much on one or other of the theories of what is happening in UFO encounters. However, one other classification system has been making gains on Hynek's old categories. This is the Vallee Classification System (VCS), devised by the French UFOlogist Jacques Françis Vallee. A graduate of Hynek's astronomy course at Northwestern University, Vallee is one of the leaders of the European 'psychosocial' school of UFOlogy. However, Vallee devised a system that can be used by any of the competing factions within UFOlogy.

Vallee's system looks at three main aspects of UFO reports and classifies them under three categories: Fly-Bys (FB), Manoeuvres (MA) and Close Encounters (CE). Close Encounters is the 'highest' category while Fly-Bys is the 'lowest'. Each of these categories is subdivided into five subcategories:

Fly-bys (FB)

- FB1 – UFO is seen flying in a straight line.
- FB2 – UFO is flying in a straight line that leaves behind physical evidence.
- FB3 – Fly-by with alien beings seen on board.

UFOs: a close encounter of the second kind.

- FB4 – Fly-by with the witness experiencing a sense of altered reality.
- FB5 – Fly-by that results in injury or death.

Manoeuvres (MA)
- MA1 – UFO seen travelling in an erratic manner.
- MA2 – UFO manoeuvres causing physical effects.
- MA3 – UFO manoeuvring with alien beings seen on board.
- MA4 – UFO seen travelling in an erratic manner with the witness experiencing a sense of altered reality.
- MA5 – UFO manoeuvres that cause injury or death.

Close Encounters (CE)
- CE1 – UFO comes within five hundred feet of the witness, but they feel no effects.
- CE2 – UFO comes within five hundred feet of the witness and leaves traces of landing or injures the witness.
- CE3 – UFO comes within five hundred feet of the witness with alien beings visible.

- CE4 – The witness is abducted.
- CE5 – Abduction that results in permanent injury or death.

Within each of these subdivisions, cases are graded according to their intensity, the amount of detail given and their effects on the witness. Then each report is also given a credibility score based on three other criteria: the reliability of the source, the thoroughness of the investigation of the sighting, and possible explanations.

The Vallee system is much more complex that Hynek's classification, but this simply reflects the increasingly complicated nature of the UFO phenomenon. And it does have the advantage of retaining the old 'close encounters' category.

Natural Causes

Most UFO researchers agree that the majority of flying saucer sighting reports can be dismissed as misperception, misidentification of unusual aerial events, such as meteorological effects, and downright hoaxes. When those cases are set aside there are still a large number of events in the skies that cannot be accounted for by normal means. But there is now a growing body of UFOlogists, especially in Europe, who seek to explain many of these genuine sightings, not as alien spacecraft, but as the result of a hither-to-unidentified natural phenomenon. Their theory is that these genuinely unidentified objects are so-called 'earthlights', thought to be produced by fault lines in the earth's crust.

For many years, the idea that earthlights – sometimes called balls of light (BOLs) – lies at the heart of the UFO phenomenon has been shunned by mainstream UFOlogy, which concentrated almost exclusively on the idea that UFOs were alien spacecraft. However, the early explorer of the unexplained, Charles Fort (1874-1932), who gave his name to 'Fortean phenomena', was among the first to observe that strange 'meteors' appeared to coincide with earth tremors and earthquakes. Bu it was only in the 1960s, after the discovery of tectonic plates, that several UFOlogists took the next step and began to correlate UFO sightings and geological fault lines.

French researcher Ferdinand Lagarde found that at least forty per cent of low-level flying saucer sightings occurred over, or close to, fractures in the earth's crust. Veteran American UFOlogist John Keel also began to look at the association between the appearance of unusual lights and areas of faulting and anomalies in the earth's magnetic field.

In the 1970s, earth-mysteries researchers Paul Devereux and Andrew York mapped strange phenomena reported over the centuries in the English county of Leicestershire and found that both meteorological anomalies – such as 'strange lightning' – and UFO sightings occurred most often over the fault-line regions of the county.

In 1977 Dr Michael Persinger, a neuroscientist and geologist, then at Laurentian University in Canada, and researcher Gyslaine Lafreniere published a study of the United States that pointed to a correlation between high levels of UFO activity and the sites of earthquake epicentres. Persinger and Lafreniere theorised that UFOs were electromagnetic phenomena arising from magnetic fields in the atmosphere caused by the squeezing of rocks under pressure. This is related to the scientifically respectable piezoelectric effect, by which certain crystals give off electricity when squeezed or distorted. In the run-up to an earthquake, tremendous energy would be generated by tectonic stress distorting the mineral crystals found in the earth's crust.

Possible ball lightning photographedin the summer of 1978 by Werner Burger at Sankt Gallenkirch, Vorarlberg, Austria.

There could be other natural mechanisms at work here too. Light can be produced when enormous forces crush certain crystals. When the earth's tectonic plates move against each other the friction also generates an enormous amount of heat. Water in the surrounding rock would be vaporised. It would become ionised, collect around the fault and be expelled as luminous plumes of ionised plasma into the air above.

Normally these naturally occurring crustal forces would operate evenly over very large geographical regions and without having a visible effect. But at times of tectonic stress, these forces could become focused in a few small areas of particular geological resistance or instability – such as fault lines, mineral deposits, stubborn rock outcrops, hills and mountains – where the electromagnetic forces generated would produce strange airborne lights. This idea was tested experimentally in Boulder, Colorado, by the US Bureau of Mines, who filmed rocks with high crystalline content as they were placed under stress and allowed to fracture. Prior to this shattering, what looked like mini UFOs were created in the laboratory due to chemical and electrical charges emitted by the rock. This was the first demonstration of what has come to be known in UFOlogy as the Tectonic Strain Theory, or TST.

Devereux has pointed out that, if you scaled up the Boulder experiment to the size of mountains, it would produce enough earthlights to explain the UFO activity you see in 'window areas', which are invariably areas of tectonic stress. In 1982, he applied this theory to his study of sightings in the UK's most active UFO window in the Pennine Hills.

Dr Persinger continued his research and further explored and refined the TST theory. In 1986, he was joined geologist by John Derr in a study of a wave of lights seen over the Yakima Indian Reservation, Washington State. During the 1970s, firewardens on the reservation photographed huge orange balls of light hovering above rocks. They had also seen smaller ping-pong-sized balls of light dancing along ridges. The area had long been prone to unusual meteorological effects, such as glowing clouds.

Derr and Persinger discovered that the lights appeared most

often along the ridges that cut across the reservation. These were riddled with fault lines. They also appeared around Satus Peak. Here a fault line broke the surface at the site of one of the strongest earthquakes that occurred in the region in the thirteen years covered by their study. Another wave of sightings occurred in the seven months before a big earthquake that occurred while Derr and Persinger were at work.

The significance of the Yakima study is that the reservation is in the foothills of the Cascade Mountains where, in 1947, Kenneth Arnold saw the first flying saucers –nine glittering objects flying in formation over a mountain ridge. This made a strong tie between 'earthlights' and UFOs.

A second study that made that connection occurred in the remote valley of Hessdalen in Norway. Hessdalen is seventy miles southeast of the remote northern town of Trondheim. The region is rich in copper and other metals. In November 1981 the people in the isolated farms in the valley saw strange yellow and white lights. They appeared just below the summits and ridges of the surrounding mountains. Along with regular balls of light, they saw inverted Christmas trees and bullet-shaped lights with the pointed end downwards. The farmers also heard underground rumblings and saw flashes in the sky.

As the phenomena were clearly linked with UFOs, the Norwegian Defence Department was called in. In March 1982 two Royal Norwegian Air Force officers turned up in Hessdalen to study the situation. By the summer of 1983, sightings had become increasingly frequent. They became big news in Scandinavia, but the Norwegian Defence Department came up with no explanation. Suspecting another official cover-up, Norwegian and Swedish UFO groups pooled their resources and set up Project Hessdalen. From 21 January to 26 February 1984 activity in the valley was monitored twenty-four hours a day with a range of specialist instruments, including radar – even though temperatures dropped as low as minus 30 degrees Celsius. Nevertheless the team managed to capture numerous strange lights on film and pick them up on radar. This sometimes proved baffling. On one occasion, several members of the team noticed a strange undulating sensation in their chests when the lights appeared. In another case, a bright light was seen travelling across the sky. But although it appeared constant to the naked eye, it appeared on the radar screen only every second sweep.

More earthlights were seen in the US when local newspaper reporter John Bennett heard reports that crowds of people were going to watch displays of strange lights at a ranch outside the town of Ada, seventy miles south-east of Oklahoma City. Deciding to investigate for himself, Bennett drove out to the remote ranch that afternoon. He parked his car and waited. As dusk approached, he saw an orange light appear in the middle of some trees. At first, he thought it was the lights of a house. But he changed his mind when the glowing orb started growing steadily larger until it was about three feet across. Then it began darting back and forth, changing colour as it did so. Suddenly a piece broke away and started bouncing across the field in front of him.

Project Hessdalen researched mystery lights in Norway.

'It looked like a luminous basketball,' said Bennett.

After some time, the light went out. Another witness told Bennett that he had seen another light earlier that had come right up to the fence where he was standing.

'I didn't move, and it was like it was looking right at me,' he said.

Light phenomena are frequently reported along the San Andreas Fault in California, and in 1973 a strange streak of light was photographed over the Pinnacles Mountain Monument nearby by physicist David Kubrin. As it moved it created shock waves. Then it stopped dead and began to spin before dissolving. What amazed

Kubrin was that it had exhibited signs of having mass – by producing shock waves – but somehow managed to stop without
decelerating.

In 1989, geochemist Paul McCartney published his report of his
investigation into the appearance of earthlights in north-west Wales
in 1904 and 1905. Balls of red light were seen at various sites, but
showed up most regularly over the field next to the chapel in
Llanfair. He traced the sightings on a map and found that they ran
down the course of the Mochras Fault that runs out into Tremadog
Bay. Similar lights were seen in many parts of Wales during a wave
of earthquake activity that lasted from 1892 to 1906. The area lies
next to the Lleyn Peninsula which is one of the UK's most active
earthquake areas. In July 1984, it was the epicentre of an earthquake measuring 5.5 on the Richter Scale. The lights reappeared
briefly. The evening before the earthquake local people saw a brilliant white light, said to be the size of a small car, float in from the
sea and land on the beach.

Then between 1 November 1988 and 21 January 1989
researchers from Quebec University made fifty-two sightings of
strange light while on a seismic monitoring expedition to the
Saguenay/Lake St John region of south-east Canada. Balls of light,
both stationary and moving, were seen several hundred feet up in
the air, some persisting as long as twelve minutes. And fireballs up
to ten feet in diameter repeatedly popped out of the ground – sometimes only a few yards away from the observer. This research team,
again, linked these UFO-type phenomena to rising tectonic strain
in the ground that led up to an earthquake in the area.

The link between earthlights and UFOs has split the world of
UFOlogy in two. The old-guard UFOlogists continue to advocate
the extraterrestrial spacecraft theory and argue that small balls of
lights can hardly explain solid-bodied craft that are seen in daylight
– or, indeed, the sixty per cent of UFO sightings that do not occur
near fault lines. On the other side of the fence are the new model
earthlight researchers who point out that the phenomenon is not
confined to small balls of light. With an appropriate build up of
energy, earthlights can reach the size of a conventional flying-

saucer. And they contend that, if earthlights are made from some kind of plasma – hot, electrically charged gas – they would also appear shiny and metallic in daylight, explaining the 'silvery discs' reported by Kenneth Arnold and many other witnesses.

To resolve the argument one way or the other, more data is required. A new Project Hessdalen has been set up in Norway and an expedition is planned to the Australian outback, where there has been persistent earthlight activity. Meanwhile, a research group headed by Paul Devereux has shown that geomagnetic anomalies and sightings of dancing lights around the increasingly active volcano, Popocatapetl, in Mexico have coincided with that country's recent prolonged UFO 'flap'.

'The fact is that the vast majority of UFOs are described as balls of light,' says Devereux. 'But it's only subjective interpretation that turns them into the lights of an alien craft.'

However, some consider this research, no matter how fascinating, as a diversion from the real business of UFOlogy – finding aliens.

More Windows

Paul Devereux's work on UFO window areas has opened the way to even more exotic theories. It has long been noted that window areas tend to feature not only UFOs but also other sorts of strange phenomena, including monster sightings and time anomalies. This has led John Keel to suggest that windows are portals between our reality and a supernatural dimension. He believes these represent points of weakness in the boundary between the two realities that allow strange phenomena to flow into our world – and possibly take us in the opposite direction. This would explain alien abduction and mysterious disappearances. If a window is the result of natural physical energies induced into the atmosphere by local geological factors, then they should remain relatively constant across time. So a window area would not only produce modern-day UFO sightings, but also reports of strange phenomena down the centuries. Deveraux's study of the historical records shows that the Pennine Hills is just such a window.

At the centre of the window on the Yorkshire–Lancashire border is the UK's most UFO-plagued town – Todmorden. It boasts dozens of sightings and six alien contact cases – out of just a hundred in the whole of the UK. In one case, a policeman from Todmorden was being abducted, but while he was being dragged into the UFO his boot caught on something and split.

Another case involved children's home worker Jenny, who was on her way home after horseback riding on the hills around Walsden. As she walked down the steep path from the moors to the town, she noticed that her dog was looking up into the sky. She look upwards to see what it was looking at and saw a lens-shaped object with coloured light under it floating silently at around roof-top height. As she stood and stared there was a telepathic exchange of information between her and the occupants of the UFO.

'It was like being plugged into a computer,' she said.

Contact ended when the UFO split into three separate glowing pieces and shot off in different directions.

UFOlogist Peter Hough has spent over twenty-five years studying the Pennine window and has come to the conclusion that we live in a multiverse, where other dimensions intersect with our own.

'Certain areas act as access points,' he says.

However, there may be a more prosaic explanation. Fiery balls of light appeared above the ancient church in the village of Linley, Shropshire. At the same time, the locals reported the presence of a poltergeist. Metal door latches opened themselves, crockery moved by itself and chairs were hurled across the room. Dr Michael Persinger says that earthlights might also be triggered by a localised increase in the Earth's magnetic field, which would explain these other bizarre happenings.

Abductions Experts

Although there have been numerous well-documented cases of alien abductions since the 1960s, many UFOlogists refuse to believe then. So in an attempt to discover whether they were really happening, in June 1992, the first Abduction Study Conference was held at the Massachusetts Institute of Technology. Three of the world's leading experts attended. They included Budd Hopkins, a pioneering investigator in this field, and Dr David Jacobs, associate professor of history at Temple University, who had been investigating UFOs for twenty-five years.

Chairing the conference was Dr John E. Mack, professor of Psychiatry at Harvard Medical School and a Pulitzer Prize winner. He was also a founder of the psychiatry teaching department and Cambridge Hospital, Harvard, and director of the Program for Extraordinary Experience Research at the Center for Psychology and Social Research.

The conference concluded that, although people from a whole cross-section of society had been abducted, their reports showed a remarkable consistency. The same type of aliens were involved in most cases. The abduction procedures were the same and abductees reported similar details of what they were subjected to. If alien abduction was some form of delusion, the accounts should differ wildly. Yet they showed consistent and repeated patterns. This was strong evidence that victims really were being abducted.

Greys were almost always responsible, though in some cases they are directed by taller humanoid aliens. Victims found themselves under the total control of the aliens. Inside the craft, they were forced to strip, made to lie on a table and subjected to intimate examinations and invasive surgery. Victims were then returned, though usually their memories had been wiped clean of the events, which could only be accessed through regressional hypnosis.

Added to that, Professor Mack pointed out, the victims often had hard physical evidence of their abduction. People returned with scars on their bodies that were fully healed though they were not been there before the abduction. Strange implants have been located on X-rays and CAT scans. Some have been removed and examined.

Chemical analysis of the implants has shown that they were usually made from elements found on Earth. But one of Professor Mack's colleagues, a nuclear biologist, ran tests on an implant taken from the nose of an abductee and discovered that the implant was not a naturally occurring biological structure. It was made

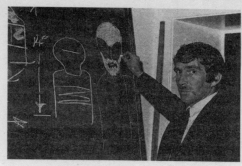

PC Alan Godfrey, who in November 1980 was allegedly abducted into a UFO at Todmorden, West Yorkshire.

from manufactured fibre. Leir's work on isotope ratios had not been done at this time.

The leading sceptics also turned up at the conference. They dismissed the physical evidence provided by Professor Mack and others, and claimed that no reliable evidence for abduction exists outside the victim's imagination. The villain of the piece, according to the sceptics, was the use of regressional hypnosis techniques to recover hidden memories. The Society for Psychical Research's Kevin McClure claimed that the abduction researchers using hypnosis are not qualified psychologists. When they did use qualified ones, McClure said, they implanted memories. He alleged that, under hypnosis, victims were encouraged to recount details that support the abduction scenario by asking leading questions.

McClure also argued that False Memory Syndrome may also be to blame. This is a disorder where the subconscious creates a bogus memory to cover up some painful childhood trauma such as sexual abuse. Abductees may be subconsciously creating false memories of an alien abduction to protect themselves from the real memories of a more traumatic experience.

Professor Mack, a psychologist by training, dismissed this theory.

Painting by Dr Susan Blackmore of a hypnotising alien.

'There is not a single abduction case in my experience or that of other investigators that has turned out to have masked a history of sexual abuse or any other traumatic cause,' he said. 'In fact, the reverse has frequently occurred – that an abduction history has been revealed in cases investigated for sexual or other abuse.'

Psychologist Susan Blackmore of the University of the West of England had another theory. She claimed that an abduction experience could be induced artificially by stimulation of the temporal lobes – the part of the brain where memories are stored. A Canadian research team under Dr Michael Persinger from the University of Sudbury, Ontario, supported this thesis. They had designed a helmet that generated a magnetic field. Dr Persinger claimed that, when this field was applied to the back of the brain, it could produce an alien abduction experience in people who have never previously claimed to have had one. But when the device was tried out on Dr Susan Blackmore, she said she felt 'someone pulling my arms and legs' and 'sudden and uncontrollable emotions'. This is hardly an alien abduction experience.

The author of *Allergies and Aliens*, Albert Budden, also said that electromagnetic fields create memories of alien abductions. He was convinced that the wave of abduction reports over the last forty years is caused by electromagnetic pollution. Electromagnetic radiation in the atmosphere is strong enough to affect the temporal lobes of abductees' brains, he says, causing abduction-like experiences. All abductees are electrically hypersensitive, he believes, and their experiences are a symptom of their allergic reactions to electromagnetic fields in the environment.

But Hopkins, Jacobs and Mack pointed out that over-active imaginations, false memories and electromagnetic simulation of temporal lobes cannot explain physical scars on abductees' bodies or the implants taken from them.

Dr Sue Davidson, a psychotherapist, thinks all abductees are raving mad. 'I have not come across the phenomenon of abduction by aliens except as a delusional belief of someone suffering from schizophrenia,' he says. But how does that explain cases like that of Travis Walton, where there were other witnesses to the 'space-napping'? Are they all mad? If they are then it is an insanity that is widespread in society. In 1995, Robert Durant compiled the statistics on alien abductions. He discovered that some five million Americans had reported having been abducted over the previous fifty years. That works out at about 274 a day. Assuming that it takes six aliens to abduct a human – abductees rarely report that they have seen more than six – and that each six-alien team abducted twelve humans a day, you would need just 137 to cover the whole of America.

And UFOlogists have now tied the alien abductions to the mutilation of livestock as further evidence that aliens are conducting genetic experiments planet-wide. Again, bizarrely butchered carcasses are not caused by hallucinations, delusions or false memories.

Alien of the Soul

So how do the earthlight theorists explain the phenomenon of alien abduction? It might not be as hard as you think. Let's look at one of the most celebrated alien abduction cases in the whole of UFOlogy – that of Travis Walton, whose abduction formed the basis of the 1993 movie *Fire in the Sky*.

Walton was abducted one November evening in 1975, from a forest track near his home in Heber, Arizona. A lumberjack, he was travelling home with the rest of the wood-cutting crews in the truck, tired after a long day's work, when, in a clearing up ahead, they saw a strange, glowing ball of light. As the truck came closer, Walton jumped out and rushed towards the mysterious object, which cast a ring of light on the ground. It was about twenty feet across and floated in the air unsteadily, emitting strange beeping and rumbling sounds.

A blue-green bolt of light zapped out of the object. Walton heard a crackling sound and felt 'a numbing shock… like a high-voltage electrocution'. It lifted him up and flung him to the ground. The rest of the crew fled. By the time they returned to the scene, the mysterious ball of light was seen shooting skyward, and Walton had disappeared.

Five days later, Walton turned up naked in a phone box. He was

seriously dehydrated, delirious, dazed, distraught and half-dead.
He had been knocked out by the bolt of light. Later he recalled
regaining consciousness in some sort of spacecraft, surrounded by
'foetus-like' aliens, with large dark eyes and marshmallowy skin.

It certainly seemed that something odd had happened in the
woods the evening he went missing. But had Walton had an
encounter with an earthlight rather than an alien spaceship?
Certainly what Walton and his workmates saw was the right size
and shape to be an earthlight. And reports from around the world
of earthlights mention that they make strange sounds, just like the
ones Walton and his workmates had heard.

As earthlights are an electromagnetic phemonemon, one could
easily have zapped him with a bolt of electricity. If Walton had suffered a massive electric shock, he might have been left in a confused mental state. He could have wandered off into the forest and
lost himself there for days. In that case, what were the strange
aliens Walton recalled?

According to Canadian neuroscientist and earthlight proponent
Dr Michael Persinger, an individual exposed to enormous electromagnetic fields is likely to experience a number of effects on his or
her body, brain and mind. These effects could include impaired
memory and vision. At its most extreme, an electromagnetic field
might put a victim into a trance-like state where the boundaries
between waking and dreaming become blurred and they might suffer intense hallucinations.

The area of the brain most sensitive to changes in magnetic and
electrical fields is the area of the temporal cortex. Under the cortex
proper lie the amygdala and hippocampus. Stimulation of the
amygdala produces intense emotional feelings, while alterating the
function of the hippocampus can modify memory and release
dreams into the waking state.

In an effort to explain alien abductions, Michael Persinger has
been running a series of experiments in which volunteers have the
temporal cortex of their brains subjected to magnetic fields.
Subjects sit in a darkened soundproof cubicle, wearing a helmet
that creates magnetic 'vortices'. Computer-controlled electrodes

directed these into various areas of the temporal cortex with great precision. During the course of the experiment, subjects see visions or feel some sort of presence. One even said the cubicle was haunted by the devil himself.

Persinger has found that when a subject has undergone several of these sessions, it takes little to trigger what he calls 'the mystical state of mind'. The magnetic helmet often induced vivid scenes from infancy and childhood.

Journalist Ian Cotton tried this out. He found himself sitting in a darkened cubicle with a magnetic helmet on. The first thing he was conscious of was a strange noise, then he went into a lucid dream state. He said that it was as clear as if his 'inner eye' was a video camera, and he saw vivid scenes from his childhood. He saw the pattern of the wallpaper in his bedroom and the red roses on the tablecloth in his childhood home, along with other long-forgotten details, with lifelike clarity.

In one particularly telling experiment, the subjects were asked concentrate on a single light in front of them. It was a normal sixty-watt electric light bulb, but many subjects described seeing slit-mouthed, grey-skinned aliens and horrific medical probes – images common to the typical UFO abduction scenario.

Medical researchers who have conducted experiments with psychedelic substances such as dimethyltryptamine (DMT) and LSD have had similar effects. Drugs induce vivid hallucinations and infantile regression with some people even claiming to have re-experienced their own birth trauma. As well as occurring in certain vegetables and seeds, DMT occurs naturally in the body. Native American tribes take it as a means of seeing spirits, contacting dead ancestors or communicating with the gods. Modern users of the drug find themselves in a deep mental state, where they see primitive creatures not dissimilar to Grey aliens. One research subject also reported being escorted by alien entities to a kind of landing platform at a space station. There he met android-like creatures that were 'a cross between crash dummies and the Empire troops from *Star Wars*'. Another said they saw a 'giant, complex control panel' and creatures that were 'bipedal and roughly human size'. These are all familiar images from abductions.

According to UFO researcher Alvin Lawson, the archetypal image of the Grey alien inhabits this very realm of our imagination. It is a kind of primal template of the mammal. Lawson says that the Grey, with it large eyes, tiny features and a small, wasted body, is essentially an elaborate image of the human foetus and as such is an archetype lodged deep within our minds. Certainly, the image of a baby is closely associated with the Greys, who are the most common abductors. Women regularly report that the aliens take their babies and, more commonly, their foetuses. Many abductees, men as well as women, report aliens probing their reproductive organs. And UFOlogist Dennis Stacy says that the Grey abduction motif is associated with the trauma surrounding abortion.

A number of researchers now believe that the alien abduction experience can be triggered by a variety of temporal lobe stimuli in those with sufficient sensitivity. This sensitivity can have been induced by trauma – either a physical trauma such as an electric shock or a psychological trauma such as an incident of child abuse. Such stimuli sensitise the temporal cortex. What's more, they are cumulative, each one leaving the subject more susceptible the next time.

British investigator Albert Budden has interviewed numerous abductees, and found that virtually all of them have suffered such trauma. Electrical sensitivity is common among them. When such people come within the influence of high-tension wires, for example, the electromagnetic field can precipitate hallucinations of such vividness that they think they really have encountered a UFO or aliens.

Abductees usually end up back in their own bed. Companions are not aware that they have been missing and abductees often feel that they have been abducted in some abstract or spiritual sense, while their body has been left behind in bed. Finnish abductee Rauni-Leena Luukkanen-Kilde said that during her abductions it was her 'astral' body that boarded the spaceship. The scars that manifested themselves on her physical body later appeared as a result of the trauma to her spiritual self, she thought.

Alien Races

The Grey alien became the best known species of extraterrestrial when alien abductee Whitley Strieber put the picture of one on the cover of his 1987 best-seller *Communion*. However, despite the enduring fame of the Grey, on the night he was first abducted, 26 December 1985, Strieber actually encountered three other types of creature.

One was the robot-like being that initially led him out of the bedroom of his country home in upstate New York. Then, in the forest outside, he encountered a large number of short, stocky beings in dark blue overalls. They had wide, blue faces, 'glittering, deep-set eyes', pug noses and broad, human-like mouths, he said. It was only later, when he found himself inside the circular room, that he encountered Grey-like beings – but their eyes, although black, were not almond shaped but 'as round as buttons'.

Strieber's case is by no means unique. While virtually every abduction case involves Greys, abductees regularly see a variety of aliens during their experiences. Dutch therapist Hilda Musch made a survey of abductees in the Netherlands and found that 85 per cent of them reported encounters with aliens other than Greys. Numerous different types have been reported since contact with extraterrestrials began. Sceptics say that there are as many types of alien as there are people who report them. But that is not entirely true. Contact reports do show some degree of consistency. In fact, all the aliens reported being seen over the past century can be categorised into one of four classes:

1. **Humanoid** – These are essentially human in shape, though witnesses have the strong sense that they are not human. This class includes Greys.

2. **Animalian** – These are animal-like creatures, including reptilian aliens and Chupacabras.

3. **Robotic** – These are entities that have a distinctly mechanical appearance.

4. **Exotic** – This is a catch-all category for those that do not fit into any of the categories above, and makes up just five per cent of the sightings.

Each class of alien can be further divided into types. The most recognisable type of Humanoid is called the Human. This is simply because it is nearly impossible to tell 'them' from 'us' – except they are usually better looking with blond hair and blemish-free complexions. These 'Nordic' types used to be very common visitors to Earth. They were the aliens who visited George Adamski first on 20 November 1952, landing somewhere between Desert Center, California and Parker, Arizona. They had long blond hair, high foreheads and seemed to radiate great love, warmth and understanding.

Then there are the familiar 'Short Greys', which are the main alien type seen on Earth. Before they were made famous by Whitley Strieber, they had made an appearance at the end of the movie *Close Encounters of the Third Kind*. This, UFO sceptics said, would spark a rash of copycat sightings. It did not happen. Short Greys had already appeared in movies in the 1940s and 1950s. They were the pilots of the flying saucers that crashed at Roswell in 1947. But in the literature they predated that, first

'Grey' alien entity, as portrayed by Rod Dickinson; oil canvas, 7ft x 7ft.

appearing on the cover of the magazine *Astounding Stories* in 1935.

Greys are often not very nice. But as astronomer Carl Sagan once remarked: 'I would love it if there were aliens here, even if they are a little short, sullen, grumpy and sexually preoccupied.'

Closely related are Short Non-Greys. They are like Greys but they are very hairy or have green skin and are common visitors to Latin America. It was a pair of the Green race that geologist Rapuzzi Johannis encountered when out studying rock formations in northern Italy on the night of 14 August 1947. They were about three feet tall and had green faces. When they came within six feet of him, Johannis noticed their hands. They had eight jointless, opposable fingers. Small green Short Non-Greys appeared in the movie *Invasion of the Saucermen* in 1957.

The Animalians also include some creatures that are not formally thought of as extraterrestrials – such as Yetis, swamp creatures and goblins. Bigfoots, for example, show all the characteristics of being alien. Some even have spaceships. Stephen Pulaski and two boys came across a dome-shaped craft that had landed near Greensburg, Pennsylvania, on 24 November 1973. Suddenly, two large, bear-like creatures appeared. They were eight feet tall with glowing, yellow-green eyes. Being a good American, Pulaski pulled a gun and shot at them. It had no effect. The boys then fled. Pulaski gave them covering fire, to no avail.

Abductee Betty Andreasson saw an entirely different type of Animalian. When she was abducted from her home in South Ashburnham, Massachusetts, on 25 January 1967, she was taken on a saucer-shaped craft to some other world where she saw three-feet high lemur-like creatures. They were headless and had eyes on the ends of prehensile stalks.

Robotic aliens come in just two types. The most common is the Metallic, which is mechanical and made totally out of metal. Lee Parish of Prospect, Kentucky, saw three machine-like beings on 27 January 1977. Under hypnosis, he said that two of the slab-like creatures were six foot tall. One of them was bulky and white, the other slim and red. The third towered above the others. It was around twenty feet tall and black. Scottish forester Bob Taylor is also thought to have encountered Robotic aliens in 1979 when he was attacked by two metal beach balls around a foot in diameter with six legs that emerged from a UFO. He smelt a pungent odour before passing out. There is also a rare type of Robotic alien that has parts made out of a substance that resembles flesh. They are called Fleshy Robots.

The Exotic category of aliens again has two main types. The Apparitional are at least partially transparent, while the Physical are completely solid. Hans Gustafsson and Stig Rydberg encountered a Physical Exotic while out driving near Domesten in Sweden on the night of 20 December 1958. They noticed a glow in the woods and stopped to investigate. In a clearing, they saw a spacecraft with four odd-shaped creatures jumping around the landing site. The amorphous, blue-green blobs were six feet tall and hostile. The two men barely escaped the suction force of the blobs' onslaught.

Aliens are a mixed bunch and several types often appear together. In May 1969 Brazilian soldier Jose Antonio was abducted by two short aliens in silver suits. On board their craft he met another alien who was about four feet tall with wavy, waist-length hair, large eyes, a mouth like a fish and deep-set greenish eyes. And in July 1983, Ron and Paula Watson encountered four aliens in Mount Vernon, Missouri – two silver-suited humanoids, a Bigfoot with shaggy hair all over its huge body and a 'lizard man'.

That there is an enormous variety of aliens is no real surprise. After all, there is a huge variety of life on earth. And alien visitors are hardly a rarity. Huge numbers of aliens have dropped in. An American survey found that some five million people have been abducted by aliens over the past fifty years – almost three hundred a day. It is estimated that the average abduction team comprised six aliens. From the length of time each abduction takes, it has been worked out that they can perform a maximum of twelve abductions per day. That means that 140 aliens have to be at work day and night to cope with the workload in the US alone.

Lizard Men

The lizard man Ron and Paula Watson saw was six foot tall, with green reptilian skin, webbed hands and feet, and glowing, cat-like eyes with vertical pupils. This was a sighting of a reptilian alien. Indeed these 'reptoids' are the most common species of alien after the Greys, and, for that reason, the most fascinating.

One was seen in Italy on 6 December 1978. Twenty-six-year-old night-watchman Fortunato Zanfretta saw four bright lights moving behind a house at Marzano in Genoa. He went to investigate and was confronted by a nine-feet-tall bipedal reptoid, which pushed him to the ground and then vanished. Zanfretta picked himself up and ran to his car. On the way, he felt a sudden heat, heard a loud whistling sound and saw a huge triangular craft soaring up into the sky. He radioed his colleagues for help and, when they arrived, he took them to where the craft had taken off. There, they found a depression the ground. It was twenty-five feet across and shaped like a giant horseshoe.

Under hypnosis, it was discovered that Zanfretta had been abducted by the reptoid and taken on board its craft for a time. He could not remember much about the spacecraft's interior, but he gave a vivid description of the alien. It had horn-like projections on its forehead above luminous-yellow, triangular eyes, pointed spines on either side of its head and a stocky body. Its skin was dark green and marked by a series of horizontal folds or ribbing.

Numerous UFOlogists have collected reports of similar sightings. 'When a so-called reptilian is repeatedly described as having the same scaly skin, claws for fingers, and extreme interest in sexuality, one must pay attention,' said Dan Wright at MUFON's 1995 symposium in Seattle.

In the autumn of 1938, near the town of Juminda in Estonia, two eyewitnesses saw a three-foot high creature with greenish-brown skin. It had slit-like eyes and month and looked like a giant frog, they said. It had some trouble walking on dry land; even so, it managed to outpace the witnesses when they chased it.

On 29 June 1988 seventeen-year-old Chris Davis was driving home past Scape Ore Swamp, near the village of Bishopville in

South Carolina, at around 2 a.m., when his car had a puncture. He pulled over and changed the tyre, and was about to get back in the driver's seat, when he saw a figure running towards him across a field. As it drew closer, he saw that it was not human. Over six feet six inches tall and standing upright, it looked like a giant lizard, with green scaly skin, and slanted, red glowing eyes. It had three digits on its feet and hands, each of which had a four-inch-long black claw.

Terrified, Davis jumped back into his car. When the creature reached the vehicle it wrenched the wing mirror off in an attempt to open the door. When Davis drove off, the lizard man leapt on to the car's roof and clung on as the terrified teenager drove through the swampy wilderness at up to fifty miles an hour. Fortunately, the creature eventually lost its grip and fell off.

Davis reported the encounter to the police, and the local sheriff, Liston Truesdale, investigated. 'We checked out his reputation, and he's a pretty clean-cut kid,' said Truesdale. 'He's also agreed to take a polygraph test or go under hypnosis.'

The Lizardman of South Carolina, a strange reptilian humanoid.

Davis's father, Tommy, told the newspapers: 'All I can tell you is that my son was terrified that night. He was hysterical, crying and trembling. It took a while before he was calm enough to tell us what happened.'

In the weeks that followed, numerous other sightings were reported and Scape Ore Swamp became a media circus, with TV crews battling it out for prime filming sites. A local radio station offered a reward of $1 million for the capture of the lizard man. They kept their money. However, a number of three-toed footprints, each fourteen inches long, were later discovered in the swamp, and casts were taken. Meanwhile, numerous Fortean researchers stepped forward to offer speculative theories. Others said that Davis had been attacked by a drunken tramp who and crawled out of a ditch, and dismissed the footprints as the work of a prankster. Some later sightings indeed proved to be hoaxes and, soon, the lizard man fell out of the headlines. The enigmatic entity itself was, like so many other anomalous creatures, never identified, let alone captured.

In veteran Fortean investigator Loren Coleman's *Curious Encounters*, he reports encounters with a 'creature from the black lagoon' – named for the 1954 sci-fi cult movie – in Ohio in 1972. At around 1 a.m., on 3 March, police officer Ray Schocke was driving down a riverside road towards the town of Loveland, when his headlights lit up what he initially took to be a dog. But the creature then stood up on its hind legs and he could see that it was a three-foot tall reptilian with leathery skin and a frog-like face. The frog-man looked at him for a moment, then jumped over the guard rail, slithered down the embankment and disappeared into the river. Schocke drove to the police station and returned with fellow officer Mark Matthews. They searched the area. Although they did not find the creature, they did find scrape marks leading down to the river along the course the fleeing creature took.

Two weeks later, Matthews was driving along the same river when he saw what he took to be a dead animal lying in the road. He stopped to move the carcass. When he got out of his patrol car, the creature got up and moved to the guard rail without taking his eyes off Matthews. Matthews took a pot shot at it but missed. The creature climbed over the guard rail and made off. Other witnesses in the area reported seeing a strange frog-like creature.

That same year there were other reptilian encounters at Lake Thetis, near Colwood in British Columbia. On two separate occasions in August 1972, two sets of witnesses saw a humanoid reptile-man with a silver body covered in fish-like scales emerge from the lake. One witness said the creature had a monstrous face, huge ears, and at least one large spike projecting from its head. It was a biped, with three-pronged flippers for feet, a fish-like mouth, and very large fish-like eyes. This description fits other reptoid sightings that date back to the nineteenth century and beyond.

In 24 October 1878 a Kentucky newspaper, the *Louisville Courier Journal,* reported that a strange creature captured alive in Tennessee was on exhibit in Louisville. According to the article, the entity was around six feet six inches in height, had eyes twice as large as a human's and was 'covered with fish scales'.

Sighting reports of these creatures shows such consistency that researcher John Carpenter has been able to piece together a detailed morphology of these scaly creatures and, in MUFON's journal of April 1993, he provided an identikit so that you will recognise one if you see one. These are its characteristics:

- **Height** – six to eight feet.
- **General appearance** – grotesque, repulsive.
- **Skin** – lizard-like scales, smooth in texture.
- **Colour** – greenish to brownish.
- **Head** – central ridge running down to the snout.
- **Face** – cross between a snake and human.
- **Eyes** – cat-like with golden iris and a vertical slit for a pupil.
- **Hands** – four-fingered claw with brown webbing.
- **Chest** – external ribbing often visible.
- **Manner** – intrusive, forceful, insensitive.
- **Behaviour** – intrudes, assaults and rapes.

- **Method of communication** – none.
- **Physical evidence** – large claw marks photographed.

Some researchers have suggested that the reptoids are not new-comers to our planet. While UFOlogists speculate that Greys are a future stage in human evolution who travel back through time to visit us, some have suggested that reptoids may be a remnant of humankind's distant past. Another theory concerns human evolution. Whereas DNA shows that humankind is closely related to the higher apes, the theory of evolution cannot explain the great intellectual and cultural gap that separates *Homo sapiens* from other species. Some suggest this is because human development was spurred on by higher beings visiting our planet from outer space. During his study of reptilian aliens, UFOlogist Dr Joe Lewels turned to the Bible and other, more obscure, religious texts. He found that there are myths and religions from around world that tell of an ancient race of scaly super-beings who descended from the sky to give humankind a helping hand. Take the biblical Creation, for example. An ancient Jewish document called the *Haggadah* says that, physically, Adam and Eve were originally very different from humans today and, when they ate the forbidden fruit from the Tree of Knowledge, it says: 'The first result was that Adam and Eve became naked. Before, their bodies had been over-laid with a horny skin and enveloped with the cloud of glory. No sooner had they violated the command given them than the cloud of glory and the horny skin dropped from them, and they stood there in their nakedness and ashamed.'

The *Haggadah* also says that the snake who tempted Eve was humanoid in form. 'He stood upright on two feet, and in height he was equal to the camel.' Only after Adam and Eve's disobedience was found out was the serpent condemned to crawl on its belly. Indeed, in fifteenth century Christian art, the serpent is depicted standing on two legs and proffering the apple with an extended arm.

So the first two humans were initially covered in a shining, scaly skin, and their punishment for eating the forbidden fruit was to lose their scales. If Adam was created in the image of his maker, then his maker must have been reptilian. Support for this radical theory is found in other early documents. The *Nag Hammadi* texts, a series of ancient scrolls found inside a clay jar in a small Egyptian town of that name in 1945, contains a passage which describes what Adam and Eve did next: 'When they saw their makers, they loathed them since they were beastly forms.'

In his book *Flying Serpents and Dragons: The Story of Mankind's Reptilian Past*, reptilian researcher R.A. Boulay concludes: 'The sad fact is that in the West we have created God in our image and not the other way around. In this way we have hidden the true identity of our creators.'

Numerous researchers have also noted that the Western image of a humanoid creator is in stark contrast to the Eastern beliefs that humanity is descended from reptilian ancestors. Chinese emperors claimed lineage from a race of dragons, and certain noble Indian families claim descent from Indian serpent deities or 'nagas'. Then there is the Dogon tribe of Mali, whose astounding astronomical knowledge came from a race of reptilian extraterrestrials known as the 'Nommo'.

In his book *The Dragons of Eden: Speculations on the Evolution of Human Intelligence* Carl Sagan recalled the pioneering brain studies of Dr Paul MacLean, head of the Laboratory of Brain Evolution and Behavior of the United States' National Institute of Mental Health. MacLean's work led him to propose that the three distinct regions of the forebrain in higher vertebrates – mammals, birds and reptiles – was each acquired during a different phase of evolution. According to MacLean, the most ancient of these regions is the one that surrounds the midbrain and is known as the reptilian R-complex. This, he says, evolved several hundred million years ago and is shared by reptiles, birds and mammals. Surrounding this are the limbic system and neocortex, which both evolved later and are more highly developed in mammals. Humans experience emotions with the limbic system and think with the neocortex. But in his book *The Dreams of Dragons* biologist Dr Lyall Watson suggests that when we dream, it is our long-suppressed reptilian complex that takes over. This archaic portion of human minds might contain memory remnants of the time when, more than 65 million years ago, our ancestors, the first mammals, were tiny, shrew-like creatures that ran around the feet of the dinosaurs. It is unlikely that memories of what it was like to be a tiny creature in a world inhabited by giant reptiles would be entirely lost, even after millions of years of evolution. As our cultural memories of such things were handed down the generations as oral traditions, they would inevitably become distorted. Both Sagan and Watson suggest that this is the key to the intriguing morphological similarities between real dinosaurs and unreal dragons – and why both of these reptilian groups hold such a grip on our imaginations.

A dragon.

Dinosaurs Live

Some researchers believe that the reptilian aliens are not extraterrestrial in origin. They are the descendants of an intelligent race of dinosaurs. One such is researcher and writer John Rhodes. In his book *Dragons of the Apocalypse* he gives a detailed morphology of the reptoids. His researches have led him to conclude that the reptilian race includes a royal elite called 'Draco' – who are also reportedly working at Dulce, according to Thomas Castello. Although rarely seen, Draco are much taller that your average reptoid – up to eleven feet tall. They have cranial horns and leathery wings. He speculates that Draco may be responsible for the outbreak of sightings of 'Mothman' in West Virginia in the 1960s.

On 24 August 1995 Rhodes told the First International UFO

Congress in Mexico City that reptoids were responsible for the recent outbreak of UFO sightings there.

'They may be preparing the way for the prophesied return of the Feathered Serpent god of Mexico – Quetzalcotl,' he said.

Another believer in the survival of dinosaurs is David Barclay. But his theory is slightly different. He points out that, in the fossil records, humankind dates back only a few million years, but during that time we have evolved into an enormously intelligent species. The dinosaurs were around for 150 million years – how much higher might they have developed?

According to Barclay's book *Aliens the Answer?*, a species of humanoid dinosaurs provoked some global catastrophe at the end of the Cretaceous Period some 65 million years ago and wiped out most of its own kind, along with the more familiar species of dinosaur. But some survived. The original human beings were their pets and were bred like we breed dogs. While we evolved into *Homo sapiens* through this process, the humanoid dinosaurs evolved into Greys. This is why, Barclay says, the Greys take such an enormous interest in us.

Alien Motives

Alien abductions are widely seen as the most intriguing twist in the evolution of the UFO phenomenon. Since the first recorded case, involving the forcible abduction of Antonio Villas-Boas in 1959, an increasing number of people around the world have reported being abducted by alien entities and often subjected to humiliating medical examinations. At first their motives were puzzling, but gradually researchers are coming to understand the phenomenon.

One of the first attempts to identify the common features of the abduction experience was made by researcher Dr Thomas 'Eddie' Bullard, who began a comparative analysis of abduction cases from around the world. From his studies, he was able to identify a distinct pattern. Most abductees' experiences, he said, had eight distinct components: capture, examination, conference, tour, other worldly journey, theophany, return, and aftermath.

However, since Bullard finished his initial studies, a wealth of new abduction cases have come in and new components have been identified that may help open the way for a deeper understanding of the abduction phenomenon. One of these new components is the feeling that many abductees have that they are being controlled prior to the abduction itself. Many find themselves being attracted inexplicably to a particular place or destination by an urge they are powerless to resist.

Under regressional hypnosis, Jill Pinzarro recalled an abduction she had experienced at the age of nine in 1958. She was pushing her bicycle home from the library one afternoon, but instead of walking directly home, she found herself drawn inexplicably towards some trees. 'I didn't feel as if I could resist,' she said. Inside the trees, there was a spacecraft with a ladder. She climbed up it into an alien spacecraft where she was stripped and examined.

When she got back to the park bench, it was already dark.

Iguanadon.

She was scared, put her books in the basket on her bike and set off home. It was late and her parents were frantic. They had already called the police who were out looking for her. But when she arrived back, her parents were so relieved that they were not even angry with her.

When she was abducted again, at the age of eleven, the aliens were particularly interested in a scab on her knee she had got after falling of her bike. A tall alien stared into her eyes. She found this reassuring. The alien, she thought, really cared about her and would not let her come to any harm. But for Jill this was not accompanied by any sexual feelings. She thought the alien was a female. However, when the alien touched her on the forehead, she felt calm and had the sensation that she was willing to surrender sexually to the creature.

When she was abducted in 1980 at the age of thirty-two, she was given a baby to hold. It was about two-and-a-half-months-old, she reckoned. It had little hair and its skin was light. The alien nurse-maid said that the child needed nurturing, but they were not very good at it and they needed her to do it. The baby was quiet and seemed to enjoy Jill holding it. When she had to give it back, Jill felt an acute sense of loss. She had bonded with it. She thought this was strange because she did not consider herself a very maternal person. She had only ever wanted one child, which she had – back on Earth.

Many abductions reportedly involve the abductee being taken against their will from their house by aliens who first move them into an open area from which they are lifted at high speed by some extraterrestrial elevator into a UFO hovering overhead. Again the victim has no control over the matter.

In 1982 Barbara Archer was abducted by aliens from inside her own home. She was sixteen. One night, she had just been getting ready for bed when she noticed a light coming in through the window. She drew the curtains, but still the light seemed to illuminate the whole room. She peeked out but could see no source for the light. She checked the other window too, then got the strangest sensation that there was someone in the room with her.

By the closet she saw a small creature, which she took to be male. Although she was puzzled by the light, she was not shocked to see him there. He touched her on the wrist, which reassured her. Then she began to float straight up out of the window.

'When we went out the window, we went straight in between my house and my next door neighbour's,' she recalled. She said it was like being in a lift with no walls. She could clearly see the driveway, her house, then the rest of street, below her. She was scared of heights. It made her feel nauseous and she hoped she would not be sick.

'Up there, I could see everything. I could see all the rows of houses on my street,' she said.

She floated up underneath some sort of flying saucer. It was dark grey, metallic. Then she noticed the light was coming out of it. But the elevation continued. 'We just went right in through the bottom,' she said.

The alien she saw in her bedroom was still with her. More were waiting inside.

She also recalled being abducted when she was twelve. That time she found herself in a room with forty or fifty tables. After the regular physical examination, a tall alien came over to her and looked deep into her mind. This made her feel happy and she lay back. She did not feel sick anymore, just a little cold. Although she was scared of the smaller aliens, she liked the taller one and thought that he liked her. Again there was a very sexual element to this. Although she was only twelve, Barbara suddenly felt very womanly, very grown up. She got the feeling that the alien could read her mind and really understood her.

She was abducted again at the age of sixteen in 1982 when she was suffering from anorexia. This annoyed the aliens because she had stopped menstruating.

When she was twenty-one, Barbara went on holiday to Ireland where she was abducted again. This time the aliens got cross with her because she did not take her clothes off quickly enough. Later she was taken to a nursery on board the spacecraft, where there were about twenty babies in cribs. Some were in nappies. Others were slightly older and dressed in simple smocks. They looked kind of scary. They did not have much hair and their skin was an unnatural grey colour.

The aliens told her she could hold one and picked out a baby girl for her. The child had big eyes. They were shaped like an alien's but they were not as ugly. Barbara remembered feeling very protective and maternal. The alien nurse then told her to feed it and Barbara put the baby to her breast. Afterwards they took the baby away from her. When Barbara was told she had to leave, she felt bad leaving the baby behind. She asked the aliens whether she could see it again. They did not give her an answer.

However, it was in what the abductees observe on board the abductors' craft that researchers find the most consistency. For example, the aliens on board the UFO usually answer to the same description. Often, there is very noticeably a leader, sometimes described as a 'chief doctor' or 'captain', who seems to direct the abduction and who is generally described as a 'he'. The leader is usually described as more cold and clinical or more authoritarian than the other aliens on board. In almost all cases, he is taller than the other creatures. This started way back in 1961 when Betty Hill struck up some rapport with the taller leader.

Almost all abductees describe their captors as having large, compelling eyes. Their impenetrable blackness makes them somehow hypnotic. Some abductees feel that the aliens' eyes are a means of telepathic communication; others fear that the aliens use their eyes to exert control over abductees. However, looking into the eyes of an alien is often said to bring a soothing calmness or diminish any pain the abductee might feel.

Abduction expert David Jacobs believes that when abductees feel they have been profoundly affected by alien eyes in this way, they have, in fact, been subjected to a 'mind scan'. The aliens stare deeply into the abductee's eyes and monitor all their thoughts.

One abductee, Karen Morgan, allegedly felt the effects of 'mind scan' during her abduction in 1981. She remembered entering a UFO and being taken to a waiting area with a number of benches in arched alcoves. She sat in one and there were other men and women waiting in the others. Some wore nightclothes. One young man was slumped, as if he was not at all well. Other women looked very frightened.

They were strapped in. Karen told herself not to panic. She got the curious feeling that she had been through this before. Then the aliens came. There were two per person. The first woman was stripped. The humans were then herded into the examination room. The sick man had to be helped. Karen tried to resist but the aliens push her along anyway.

Karen was last into the examination room. There were four operating tables in the room. A shelf ran around the room with instruments on it. Karen was stripped and strapped to the table. Karen had braces on her teeth at the time and the aliens were fascinated by them. They asked her to take then out, but she refused. Next morning when she awoke, she found them on her belly.

The aliens also cut off a sample of her gum for analysis. This made her fighting mad. She asked how much more of her they were going to take and how long it took to study someone. Their answer was, it could take years.

The tall 'leader' alien asked her to look into his eyes. She did and felt that she was being overwhelmed, as if she was falling into them. Her will power was sapped. She could not look away or fight the alien in any way. It was as if she no longer had a mind of her own.

'Once you look into those eyes, you're gone. You're just gone,' she said.

Later, Karen got angry at the gynaecological procedures the alien was performing on her. She cursed the creature in her mind. The alien read her thoughts and reassured her that she would come to no harm. They performed something resembling a smear test on her, but she believed they were inserting an embryo into her, implanting it in her womb.

She found this idea repulsive and told the alien that he was not going to get away with this. He told her that she had no choice. It was part of a very important programme. But still Karen protested. She said that, back on Earth, she would have an abortion. The alien said that she would not, because she would not remember the embryo being implanted in her. She kept protesting that she would, but felt the alien's hypnotic suggestion that she would forget the incident overwhelming her mind. There was nothing to worry about, the alien said reassuringly, they had done this many times before.

Karen then remembered that she had indeed been through this procedure many times before and felt sick. The embryos, she knew, were hybrids; part human, part alien. She felt like an animal that was being experimented on. Sometimes the procedure was quick. This time it took longer because she resisted. When the alien was finished, he pulled the instruments out and patted her on the stomach. Karen was disgusted and told the alien to take his hands off her. Reluctantly, he did, but shook his head as if bewildered by her uncooperative attitude. In the morning, Karen woke back in her own bed. She found a mysterious gooey substance between her legs, took a shower and washed it off.

There are of course similarities in the events that occur on board abductors' craft as well – especially in reports of sexual and reproductive experimentation. During abductions, orgasms have reportedly been induced in both men and women, and sperm and ova have also been removed. Many female abductees claim to have been made pregnant by their captors, and then forced to carry the human–alien hybrids until the foetus is removed later, during another abduction.

Twenty-one-year-old musician Tracy Knapp recounted an experience of this nature. Knapp was driving from Los Angeles to Las Vegas with two girlfriends in 1978; she was abducted after seeing a light appear above the road and move down on top of her car. As it whizzed by them, the car started spinning. All three of them starting screaming and crying.

The car was being lifted up into the sky. Then Tracy remembered hands coming in through the window. When they touched her, she went limp. Then they lifted her out of the car. From then on, she lost sight of the other women. She did not see them again until they were back on the ground. When she returned home, she found that she was pregnant.

A few months later she was abducted again; she recalls lying down with her legs up. Two creatures were pressing on her and someone cutting her internally with long handled scissors that had very small blades. They doused the wound with a fluid that burned her. The procedure continued for a long time. The aliens seemed to be cutting threads. Then they pulled out their instruments and removed a sac with a tiny foetus in it.

'They removed something out of me. They removed a little baby or something,' she said.

This was put in a small, silver cylinder about three inches wide. The cylinder in turn was put into a drawer in the wall, along with numerous other live foetuses.

While some cases involve physical after-effects, most abductions involve some psychological disturbance. The most common is the sensation of missing time. Many abductees notice a time discrepancy between how long they perceived the encounter to have taken, and how long it had lasted in reality. These periods last maybe just a few minutes, or hours, or even, as in the case of famous abductee Travis Walton, days.

In October 1979, Luli Oswald and a companion were driving from Rio de Janeiro to Saquarema in Brazil when they saw a number of UFOs, which seemed to interfere with their car. Later, when they stopped at a service station, they found that two hours had mysteriously elapsed. Luli suffered some bad after-effects. Regressional hypnosis later revealed that they had both been abducted.

Another element regularly experienced after abductions is so-called 'screen memory'. These were first highlighted by celebrity abductee Whitley Strieber in his book *Communion*. A screen memory involves a disguised version of reality. These are used by aliens to prevent abductees remembering what actually happened. These disguises take the form of false memories or substitute images.

Debbie Jordan, the subject of UFOlogist Budd Hopkin's book *Intruders*, had a catalogue of screen memories as a result of her many abductions. On one occasion, she remembered leaving her house to visit the local store, but she was somehow 'steered' into a UFO which she saw in the store. The sales assistant in the store was a screen memory for the alien, she thought.

Professor Alvin Lawson believes that the abduction experience is a screen memory itself. It is a falsified account of the victim's birth trauma. All the elements are there, he points out. There are foetus-like creatures, obstetrics, medical equipment, even tools such as forceps. Some leave down long corridors; while some are helped out by the aliens or forcibly ejected, which he compares of a forceps birth. He compares some of the more traumatic ejections to Caesarean birth. Professor Lawson also points out the phenomenon of 'doorway amnesia'. Few abductees remember how they got into the alien craft, he says, just as no child could have any memory of how it got into the womb. The problem for Professor Lawson's thesis is that some abductees have a very clear idea of how they were conducted into the UFO.

All the elements described above occur regularly in abductions and researchers have been able establish a consistent pattern to abductions. But what light does this shed on the abduction phenomenon itself?

For some time, it has been noted that the UFO phenomena often echo ancient legends and beliefs. Instead of being abducted by gods or goblins as people were in former time, we are now taken by UFOs and aliens as if this is somehow more in keeping with the technological world that surrounds us. Following this logic, the idea has been advanced that the abduction phenomenon taps into ancient fears and concerns of human beings, expressed in the terms of today's increasingly technology-driven society. A clear parallel here can be drawn between the idea of 'alien implants' and the modern-day fear expressed in films such as *Terminator* and *Westworld* that human beings can be turned into machines.

Researcher John Rimmer argues that the recognition of authoritative figures, the feeling of being controlled and the sexual experimentation that regularly feature in the accounts of abductees all spring directly from the culture in which we live. In his book *The Evidence For Alien Abductions*, he says: 'Abduction cases grow from our own culture and social background and reflect our fears and preoccupations, both on a personal level... [and] a social level...'

Rimmer believes that the abduction experience is psychological in origin. Far from being the result of extraterrestrial intervention, abduction, he says, is a symptom of personal crisis in the life of the individual concerned. However, for abductees it is all too real.

In 1977, Professor Alvin Lawson conducted a unique experiment. He got a number of people who had no reason to believe that they had ever been abducted to write a fictional account of an imaginary abduction. When these were compared to the accounts given by real abductees there was no discernible material difference between them. This led him to conclude that the accounts of the real abductees were also fiction. Others have pointed out that this conclusion is bogus. By 1977, the major elements of the abduction experience were already well publicised and Lawson himself had given the subjects some direction. Even Lawson himself conceded that there was one huge difference between the fictional accounts and the reports of real abductees – the amount of emotion expressed. The abductees truly believed that they had undergone the abduction experience.

Bud Hopkins, who has interviewed hundreds of abductees over more than twenty years of research, performed a similar experiment. He asked subjects to imagine an abduction that involved a medical check-up. Their descriptions were nothing like abductees' reports.

'What we got was ninety per cent their last medical check-up and ten per cent *Star Trek*,' he said.

Hopkins also points out that the medical examinations reported in alien abductions are not a projection of people's health fears. Alien examinations concentrate on the reproductive system and sperm and ova extraction. Surveys show that most people are more concerned with the working of their heart and stomach.

The UFOlogists

Stanton Friedman

Nuclear physicist Stanton Friedman is one of America's leading
UFOlogists and has been researching the subject for over forty
years, ever since a one-dollar book he bought in 1959 sparked his
interest. He co-wrote *Crash at Corona* – the definitive study of the
Roswell incident –with Don Berliner. In *TOP SECRET/MAJIC*, he
investigated the Majestic-12 documents and US government
efforts to conceal evidence of alien spacecraft from the American
people. He has lectured around the world. He says that he silenced
all but a handful of sceptics who refuse to believe that the Earth is
being visited by intelligently controlled extraterrestrial spacecraft.

Curiously, Friedman has never seen a flying saucer himself.
Instead he is a critical judge of other people's reports. Nevertheless,
he says that seeing UFOs is much more common than most people
imagine. At his lectures, he asks people whether they have seen a
flying saucer. The hands go up reluctantly, he says, 'but they know
I'm not going to laugh'. Typically, ten per cent of the audience
admit to seeing a UFO. Then he asks how many of them reported it.

'I'm lucky if it's ten per cent of the ten per cent,' says Friedman.
'Sightings of flying saucers are common, reports are not.'

Friedman became interested in the world of UFOs by accident
when he was twenty-four. He was ordering books by mail and
needed to buy one more to avoid paying shipping charges. The one
he chose was *The Report On Unidentified Flying Objects* by Air
Force Captain Edward Ruppelt, former director of Project Blue
Book. Friedman read the book and was intrigued. He figured that
Ruppelt had to know what he was talking about. So he read fifteen
more books on UFOs and spent a couple of years digging up as
much information as he could.

His conclusion was that there was overwhelming evidence that
Earth is being visited by intelligently controlled extraterrestrial
spacecraft. However, he believed that, while some flying saucers

are alien space ships, most are not. He believes that since July 1947, when two crashed saucers were recovered in New Mexico along with alien bodies, the government has back-engineered spacecraft of its own. Only a few insiders know that this has been done and he calls the cover-up the 'Cosmic Watergate'.

He began investigating the Roswell incident in 1978 after being put in touch with one of the witnesses. He has now interviewed over two hundred witnesses – of those some thirty were involved with the discovery and recovery of the alien craft and the subsequent cover-up of the two crashes. On top of that he has news cuttings from Chicago to the West Coast newspapers on 8 July 1947 and FBI memos that back the story. He also believes that these show that there was a second UFO crash in New Mexico in 1947, 150 miles to the west of Corona, the first crash site, in the plains around San Augustin. He has found eyewitnesses who saw 'a large metallic object' stuck in the ground there.

He is not convinced by Ray Santilli's alien autopsy film though, seeing nothing in it that was associated with a crashed saucer at Roswell or anywhere else. He is also concerned that Santilli has refused to have the film verified. Nor has he released details of the cameraman so that they can be checked out. Friedman likes to look at the evidence.

Friedman is not flattered by being called a UFOlogist. He says that it is supposed to mean a person who has studied the science of UFOlogy, but there are no standards.

'Anybody who reads two books and carries a briefcase thinks he qualifies,' he says.

A big part of the problem of proving that flying saucers really exist is that people make wild claims that cannot be substantiated by the evidence. But he is more annoyed at the failure of the media to do their job. They have failed to dig into what Friedman considers to be the biggest story of the millennium. He believes that the media pay too much attention to what he calls the 'noisy negativists', none of whose arguments stand up under careful scrutiny, he says. 'They sound good, until you look at the evidence and they collapse of their own weight.'

He points out that there have been five large-scale scientific studies on UFOs, ten doctoral theses have been published and hundreds of papers have been produced by scientists. But most people, especially the debunkers, seem to be totally ignorant of this enormous amount of information. In his lectures he goes through the five scientific studies and asks how many people have read them. Less than two per cent of these people, who are plainly interested in the topic, are familiar with even one of the studies.

Friedman is also invited to speak to government bodies and gets a good response. But he finds that the question-and-answer sessions with the government people are a one-way street. They ask him a lot of questions but they do not reveal anything. He has spoken at Los Alamos National Laboratory and pulled a huge crowd. He has also given testimony to Congressional hearings in 1968 and at the United Nations in 1978.

Friedman finds being trained as a scientist is very useful in his work as a UFOlogist. It has meant that his approach is objective, painstaking, honest and scientific. Much of what he worked on as a scientist was classified. He wrote classified documents and had a security clearance. This gave him the opportunity to find out how security works and was good training for searching government archives for classified material later. Now he now lives in Canada and works on less sensitive science research projects such as pollution control and food irradiation.

He believes that the Majestic-12 documents prove President Harry Truman set up a super-secret group of top people from the fields of science, the military and intelligence to learn about alien spacecraft. He has spent over twelve years trawling through fifteen government archives, checking out whether these documents are real. Repeatedly, he has found confirmation of details in the documents that no one but insiders could have known. Friedman has even collected $1,000 from one critic who claimed one of the typefaces used in one of the MJ-12 documents was wrong.

'It was an absurd challenge, since I'd spent weeks searching through the government archives and he hadn't,' says Friedman. 'It also typifies the intellectual bankruptcy of the pseudo-science of anti-UFOlogy. I've yet to see a good anti MJ-12 argument.'

Friedman has had no chance to check out the data on alien abductions, but believes that every abduction story should be taken on its own merits. He has faith in abduction researchers because of his dealings with them and thinks that some people have been abducted.

According to Friedman's theory the government used five major arguments for withholding evidence from the public. The first is that it wants to figure out how flying saucers work because they make wonderful weapons delivery and defence systems. Secondly, it needs to do this before any potential enemy does. Thirdly, if this information was released, the younger generation would see humankind merely as 'earthlings' – which is what we are from an alien point of view. Friedman thinks this would be a great benefit. The problem with that is that there is no government on earth that wants its citizens to owe their primary allegiance to the planet rather than their country. Fourthly, there are certain religious fundamentalists who maintain humankind is the only intelligent life in the universe – that means that UFOs must be the work of the devil. These fundamentalists have huge political influence and their religions would be destroyed if they were proved wrong.

Finally, any announcement that the aliens were here would cause widespread panic. Some people would believe that were aliens are here to slaughter us. Others would reason that the aliens were obviously more technologically advanced than us and would bring with them new energy sources, new transportation systems, new computers and new communication systems. As a result the stock market would crash and there would be untold economic consequences.

However, Friedman still believes that the public is ready to hear the truth about UFOs. There would, of course, be some people who did not want to know – just as there are five per cent of the American public who do not believe that man has been to the moon. But the evidence about UFOs could be presented honestly and openly.

'I certainly don't think we should put technical data about flying saucers out on the table,' he says. 'But our planet is being visited by intelligent aliens. It's time we grew up.'

Jaques Vallee

Steven Spielberg's movie *Close Encounters of the Third Kind* made Jacques Vallee the most famous UFOlogist in the world. The François Truffaut character is based on the French researcher. Although he became a computer scientist for the Department of Defense, Vallee began his career as an astrophysicist. As a young man, it was curiosity that led him to study astronomy, but that same curiosity led him on into the world of UFOs. He does not find studying anomalous phenomena unscientific, pointing out that Nobel prize winner Niels Bohr said that all science starts with an anomaly.

He was working at the Paris Observatory when he first got interest in UFOs. They had observed a number of 'unidentified satellites'. However, when the scientists there were ordered to destroy the data concerning these 'anomalies' instead of sending it to their colleagues for further study, he rebelled.

This was during the early 1960s when the idea that UFOs were connected to alien intervention was widespread. Back then, he found that the 'extraterrestrial hypothesis' seemed to match witnesses' accounts. But since then, thousands more cases have been reported and statistical models could be used to analyse them. This has forced Vallee to take another, more critical look at the extraterrestrial hypothesis.

Vallee already had a passion for religious history, myths, occultism and parapsychology and, around 1968, he realised that many aspects of the UFO phenomenon were also present in the folklore of every culture. By 1975, he got the idea of combining these disciplines by considering the UFO phenomenon, not as simply a manifestation of extraterrestrial visitors, but as a control system that had been in existence since the beginning of humankind. He points out that UFO sightings did not start with Kenneth Arnold in 1947. Elements of the phenomena existed before. He believes that the wheels of Ezekiel, cherubim and burning bushes seen in biblical times, the flying goblins in luminous chariots of the Middle Ages, the phantom airships of the nineteenth century, the 'ghost rockets' of 1946 and the extraterrestrial spacecraft seen today are all essentially the same phenomenon.

As we learn more about the history and geographical distribution of the phenomenon, the standard extraterrestrial hypothesis leads to glaring contradictions, Vallee says. He believes that objects and beings connected to the UFO phenomenon are symbolic, or even theatrical, manifestations, rather than a systematic alien exploration where abductions are conducted for the purposes of so-called 'biological studies', as other UFOlogists suggest.

'We are also looking at some form of non-human consciousness,' he says. 'However, one must be wary of concluding that we are dealing with an "extraterrestrial race".'

Vallee aims to shatter the assumption that 'UFO' means 'extraterrestrial spacecraft'. He believes that behind these enigmatic luminous phenomena is a form of intelligence capable of manipulating space-time and influencing human evolution. In his best-selling book *Confrontations*, published in 1990, he analysed over a hundred UFO encounters using scientific methods, and concludes that the aliens visiting us come from another dimension.

Vallee is the champion of a bold new speculative physics. He believes that objects capable of gradually appearing and disappearing on the spot are modifying space-time topology. This validates the multidimensional models of the universe that theoretical physicists have been working on in recent years.

But he does not totally reject the extraterrestrial hypothesis, just the hard-nosed American approach to it. He believes that we share our existence with other forms of consciousness that influence the topology of our environment and affect the human mind psychically. Vallee has been accused of contradicting himself, because at times he emphasises the physical and material aspects of UFOs, while at others stressing the psychic and paranormal side. But this contradiction is in the data, he says.

Vallee is a believer in alien abduction, but believes that hypnotising abductees as practised in America is unethical, unscientific and perhaps even dangerous. He has investigated over seventy abduction cases. From his interviews with witnesses he has no doubt that the large majority of abductees have had a close encounter with an object emitting electromagnetic radiation, pulsed at hyper-frequencies. The effects on the human brain of these are unknown, so hypnotising the victims could put them at risk. He points out that UFO encounters are dangerous enough to humans as it is, with large amounts of energy confined to a restricted space.

One of the abduction cases Vallee studied was that of Franck Fontaine, who was abducted on 26 November 1979 from the Parisian suburb of Cergy-Pontoise after seeing a bright light in the sky. Vallee was particularly interested in the case because he was born in Pontoise and went to the same school as Fontaine. Although Fontaine admitted, two years later, that the abduction was a hoax, Vallee does not believe the explanations that have been given. They do not correspond to his knowledge of the area or the psychological state of the witnesses.

'I don't believe it was a UFO, but I do think that Franck was actually abducted,' he says. 'Someone is hiding something.'

The dozen or so 'implants' he has examined have not been mysterious in nature. Analysis showed that many of them were the tips of rusty needles, fragments of insects or other natural material embedded in the flesh. However, Vallee was the first to draw attention to the subject of animal mutilations over twenty years ago in his book *La Grande Manipulation* ('The Great Manipulation'), but he has not published research because he was unable to prove the link between the mutilations and the UFO phenomenon. He does believe that the link exists, though.

Vallee finds the USAF's latest explanation of the Roswell incident – that it was the crash of a balloon carrying a basket full of mannequins – laughable.

'The most recent report from the Air Force is even more absurd than all the other "explanations" given previously,' he says. 'The fact that an extremely strange object came down near Roswell and that the military made every effort to discourage research into the incident and continues to do so is beyond doubt. However, this doesn't mean that the object in question was a UFO.'

For Vallee, the jury is still out on the Roswell incident. He believes that the idea of a crash is only plausible if you believe it to be a deliberate demonstration on the part of an external intelligence. In the meantime he is investigating nineteen other different crash cases.

Vallee believes that every country's armed forces uses the UFO phenomenon to cover up operations involving advanced or illegal weapons. This started in the USSR as early as 1967, when the KGB spread rumours about UFOs in a region where the inhabitants had seen rockets being launched that were carrying satellites in violation of international agreements. UFO rumours also cloak remotely controlled rigid airships that the military use to gather electromagnetic data. An American soldier he knows approached one of these craft standing in a clearing in Germany during manoeuvres before the Gulf War and he has read US patent applications describing them.

Generally Vallee's scientific colleagues are open-minded about UFOs. They have no time for grandiose conspiracy theories, but they do admit the existence of a 'non-standard phenomenon'. During his forty years of UFO investigations, he has discovered that the UFO phenomenon is considerably more complex than he used to think. It cannot be explained simply by an extrapolation of current human technology.

'We are faced with a phenomenon that underlies the whole of human history, manipulates the real world and seems to obey laws that bear no relationship to those we hitherto imagined,' he says. 'I believe we're entering a particularly exciting period in the phenomenon's history, since we now have the opportunity of re-examining all the various hypotheses.'

More recently, Vallee has published a memoir of his years in UFOlogy called *Science Interdite* ('Forbidden Science'). This also examines the validity of the US Army's secret 'Memorandum Pentacle'.

Bob Lazar

Soft-spoken physicist Bob Lazar is one of the most controversial figures in UFOlogy. A man with a strong scientific background, he has been involved in the 'back-engineering' of alien spacecraft at the notorious Area 51 in the Nevada desert.

In 1982 he was a member of a scientific team at the US military's Groom Dry Lake installation. There he worked on a top-secret project to unravel the technology used by alien spacecraft that had been recovered from various crashes. Nine disc-shaped craft were held under armed guard in an underground section of the base known as 'S4'. The job of Lazar's team was to find out what made these flying saucers tick and whether their components could be replicated with materials found on Earth.

Many people have poured scorn on Lazar's story since it was first aired in a TV interview in 1989. As a child he was eccentric. His resumé includes bankruptcy and an association with a Las Vegas brothel. Lazar is easily discredited. Officials at Area 51 deny that anyone named Robert Lazar ever worked there – just as they once denied that Area 51 itself existed. But a salary statement issued by the United States Department of Naval Intelligence proves that Lazar did work in Area 51 for the five months as he claimed.

And when it comes to engineering, it is plain that Lazar knows what he is talking about. He has an impressive list of technical qualifications and is a scientist with a pedigree. In the early 1980s he was employed on several projects at the Los Alamos National Laboratory, New Mexico, where the first atomic bomb was developed. At Los Alamos, he conducted experiments with proton-scattering equipment and worked with high-energy particle accelerators. The work he did there was on the cutting edge of the new physics and could open the way to faster-than-light travel. As a prominent member of the town's scientific community, he earned himself an appearance on the front page of the *Los Alamos Monitor* when he installed a jet engine in a Honda CRX.

Despite the efforts made to paint him as slightly cracked, Lazar's account of what went on in Area 51 is lucid and concise, clearly not the ramblings of a disturbed mind. With his scientific background, his observations have a solid foundation. His specific task at Area 51 was to investigate the propulsion system of a small flying saucer dubbed 'the sports model', which was kept in one of the S4 hangars built into the side of a mountain. He witnessed a brief, low altitude test flight of the disc.

The sports model was some forty feet in diameter and fifteen feet high. It had three levels. The top level was an observation deck nine feet across, with portholes. Below that were the control consoles and seats, which were too small and too near the floor for adult humans to use comfortably. The main cabin had a headroom of just six feet. Also in the central level was an antimatter reactor and, located directly below it on the lower level, were the three 'gravity amplifiers', connected to the reactor by wave guides. He worked on this propulsion system both in situ in the craft and on the bench in the lab.

The power source for the sports model and the eight other discs in S4 was an 'antimatter reactor', Lazar says. These reactors were fuelled by an orange-coloured, super-heavy material called 'Element 115'. This mysterious element was the source of the 'Gravity A' wave as yet undiscovered by terrestrial science. It also provided the antimatter radiation required to power the saucer in interstellar flight.

The flying saucers in S4 have two modes of travel. For local travel, near the surface of a planet, they use their gravity generators to balance the planet's gravitational field and ride a Gravity A wave like a cork on the ocean. During interstellar travel, covering distances that would take aeons even travelling at close to the speed of light, the Gravity A wave from the nucleus of Element 115 is amplified. This bends space and time in the same way it is bent in the intense gravitational field generated by a black hole. As the saucer travels through space, time is 'bent' around the craft. By distorting space and time in this manner, the disc can travel across vast expanses of space at incredible speeds. This is the same principle used by the *Enterprise*'s 'warp drive' in *Star Trek*.

Terrestrial rockets push the craft towards their destination by blasting jets of hot gas in the opposite direct, while alien craft 'pull' the destination towards them. Lazar explains how this works with the analogy of a rubber sheet with a stone, representing the space-craft, on it. To go to any particular destination, you pinch the rubber sheet at that point and pull it towards the stone. Then, when you let got, the rubber sheet springs back, pulling the stone – or space-craft-with it.

'In a spacecraft that can exert a tremendous gravitational field by itself,' he says, 'you could sit in any particular place, turn on the gravity generator, and actually warp space and time and "fold" it. By shutting that off, you'd click back and you'd be at a tremendous distance from where you started.'

Although this type of propulsion appears to be the stuff of science fiction, many scientists believe that faster-than-light travel may be possible. Cambridge University's Lucasian professor of mathematics Stephen Hawking has suggested that interstellar travel might be achievable via natural or manmade 'worm-holes' in the fabric of space-time. Understanding how this works in practice is a bit more taxing, of course.

Inside the flying saucers' antimatter reactor, Lazar says, Element 115 is transmuted into another esoteric material called 'Element 116'. This is highly unstable and decays, releasing antimatter. The antimatter then reacts with matter inside the reactor in a total anni-hilation reaction, where one hundred per cent of the matter–anti-matter is converted into energy. This energy is used to amplify the Gravity A wave given off the Element 115 and the heat generated by reaction is converted to electricity via a solid state thermo-elec-tric generator.

The alien craft were saucer-shaped to diffuse the electrical charges generated by the antimatter reactor. In flight, Lazar says, the bottom of the alien craft glowed blue and began to hiss like a high voltage charge does on a sphere.

'It's my impression that the reason that they're round and have no sharp edges is to contain the high voltage,' says Lazar. 'If you've seen a high voltage change system's insulators, things are round or else you get a corona discharge.'

The craft's high voltage makes them hiss when they take off. Otherwise they are silent. And the hissing stops when they have climbed to twenty or thirty feet. 'There are just too many things that Lazar knew about the discs that can't be explained in any other way,' said George Knapp, the TV journalist who first interviewed him.

Lazar says that, at one time, there were Soviet scientists and mathematicians working at Area 51, alongside the Americans there. He did not know whether they were actually allowed to work on the alien craft, but believes that they were employed on the scientific and mathematical theory that underpinned his group's practical work.

They were kicked out after a major breakthrough had been made in understanding how the discs and their propulsion systems worked. They were none too happy about this. Lazar says that in the aftermath of their exclusion, paranoia at the base soared. Employees were issued with firearms, in case the Soviets tried to kidnap them.

During his time at Area 51, Lazar had to read a document the size of a telephone directory, which revealed that the top-secret base at Groom Lake was not the only US government facility back-engineering ET technology. The US government's admission that other secret bases do exist lent weight to Lazar's story. However, what goes on in them is still beyond top secret. Since Lazar's Area 51 security clearance was mysteriously revoked at the end of the 1980s, he has been subjected of intense harassment. His house and car have been broken into and he has been shot at by unseen snipers in an attempt to discourage him from divulging the secrets of S4.

Edgar Fouche

Like Bob Lazar, Edgar Fouche worked at Area 51 and has since spent his time telling the world about what is going on there. Fouche is a true insider who spent twenty-eight years with the US Air Force and Department of Defense. During that time, he was stationed at top-secret sites, including the nuclear test site in Nevada, the Nellis Test Range and the Groom Lake Air Base, home of Area 51. Fouche's work in intelligence, electronics, communications and a number of black programmes has given him inside information on some of America's most classified technological developments, including the super-secret SR-71 and SR-75 spy planes and the TR-3B, which many people believe is sometimes mistake for the 'Flying Triangle'.

However, during the 1980s when President Reagan was in power, he became completely disenchanted with the defence industry. It was full of fraud and abuse of power and he decided that he could not be associated with it anymore. He was suffering serious medical problems at the time and did not think he was going to live much longer. So he decided to speak up.

In this, he was helped by five friends who served with him in Vietnam. One was a former SR-71 spy plane pilot. Two of them went on to work for the National Security Agency. A fourth friend's father had worked for the NSA for twenty years and the fifth worked for the Department of Defense. He also gleaned information about the TR-3B by talking to pilots.

His buddy who was the SR-71 pilot told him that once, when he was flying back across the South China Sea, he saw a shadow fall across the cockpit. The aircraft started to nose down and the avionics went crazy. When he looked up to find out what was happening, he saw a UFO that was so big it completely blocked out the sun. It was oval and surrounded by a shimmering energy field, and he reckoned that it was three hundred feet across.

What really amazed Fouche was that all the pilots he spoke to reported encounters with UFOs. Some had seen circular UFOs, others had encountered plasma balls that seemed to dance around the craft. These reports were all the more impressive because the SR-71 can fly at over 60,000 feet. This gives it enormous visibility. If something is up there, an SR-71 is going to see it.

Fouche's contacts told him that the development of the TR-3B started in 1982 as part of a top-secret project named 'Aurora', whose aim was to build and test advanced aerospace vehicles. He discovered that around 35 per cent of the US government's 'Star Wars' budget had been siphoned off to finance it. The TR-3B is a triangular nuclear-powered aerospace platform and is undoubtedly the most exotic aerospace programme in existence. The designation 'TR' stands for tactical reconnaissance. This means the craft is designed to get to the target and stay there long enough pick up information on the enemy's deployment and send it back. The advantage of being powered by a nuclear reactor is that it can stay aloft for a long time without refuelling.

Its advanced propulsion system also allows it to hover silently for long periods. The circular crew compartment is located at the centre of TR-3B's triangular airframe. It is surrounded by a plasma-filled accelerator ring, called the Magnetic Field Disrupter, which generates a magnetic vortex and neutralises the pull of gravity. The MFD does not actually power the craft; what it does is effectively reduce its mass. Propulsion is achieved by three multi-mode gas-propelled thrusters mounted on each corner of the triangle. But MFD makes the aircraft incredibly light. It can fly at Mach 9 speeds vertically and horizontally, and can outmanoeuvre anything except UFOs.

One of Fouche's sources who worked on the TR-3B told him that they were working on the possibility of developing the MFD technology so that it not only reduces mass but also creates a force that repels gravity. This would give the TR-3B a propulsion system that would allow it to routinely fly to the Moon or Mars. This anti-gravity system is how UFOs work and Fouche is convinced that the TR-3B has been developed through the back-engineering of alien technology.

Fouche believes that the black triangles tracked by the Belgian Air Force in the late 1980s and early 1990s were TR-3Bs. He has a simple rule: if it is triangular it is terrestrial, if it is circular or tubular it is extraterrestrial. He says that the US government could easily get round treaty agreements that prohibit testing advanced aircraft over Europe. These agreements, he points out, say that they cannot fly an aircraft over a friendly country without that country being informed. It would be easy enough to inform the Belgian government on the sly. After all, the US is not supposed to have nuclear weapons in the UK or Japan, but they do.

Groom Lake's six-mile-long runway is the longest in the world. Fouche says that it was built to accommodate the CIA's latest super-hi-tech spy plane, the 'Penetrator' or SR-75; 'SR' stands for strategic reconnaissance. It can exceed Mach 7 with speeds of over 28,000 miles an hour at an altitude of 40,000 feet and can reach any point on the Earth within three hours. This plane is so secret that the US government does not even admit to its existence. After the SR-71 Blackbird was retired in 1990, the US Air Force said that it would not be replaced because satellites provided all the military's high-level reconnaissance needs. But Fouche's sources say that the SR-75 has been designed to service spy satellites in orbit. It acts as a 'mothership' and launches unmanned SR-74, or Scramp, craft. Operated by remote control, these can place satellites in space, reaching altitudes of 95 miles and speeds of 6,250 miles an hour, or Mach 15.

Fouche was assigned to Groom Lake in 1979 because he was one of the few people who had the necessary top-secret clearance. He was certified to work with particular equipment which, even years after the event, he was not prepared to discuss. He had been working at Nellis Air Force Base at the time and was told that he was being temporarily reassigned, but was given no idea of where he was going to be sent. Some thirty technicians were herded onto a blue bus with blacked-out windows. There were two guards on board, armed with M16 rifles. They told the passengers not to speak unless spoken to. This is how Fouche ended up at Groom Lake.

The conditions were extremely oppressive. He was issued with heavy glasses, like welders' goggles. These had thick lenses that blocked peripheral vision and prevented the wearer seeing further than thirty metres ahead. Everywhere he went, he was escorted by a soldier carrying an M16 who would never talk to him. He could not even go to the lavatory alone.

According to Fouche, the military used sinister mind-control techniques on employees. One of his five collaborators named Sal was a victim of this. A former NSA electronic intelligence expert, he had helped develop Magnetic Field Disruption. After two-years

at a top-secret NSA facility, he came down with what he thought
was the flu. He went to see the facility's doctor, who gave him
some medication and told him to go home and rest. The next day,
Sal had no memory of where he worked or who he worked for.
When his brother contacted the NSA, he was told that Sal's con-
tract had been terminated. Sal's memory has not returned and the
only evidence he has that he worked at the NSA facility at all is a
few scribbled notes and his pay slips.

Security at Area 51 was so tight that a key card and a code were
needed for every door. Fouche is very sceptical about people who
claim to have been at Groom Lake and accidentally stumbled into
a hangar with a UFO inside. His twenty-eight years with the
Department of Defense and the US Air Force taught him that anything that was top-secret was protected by numerous levels of security.

However, in Area 51 there is a facility on the Papoose Lake site
called the Defense Advanced Research Center, which extends for
ten storeys underground. It was built in the early 1980s with
Strategic Defense Initiative money. The DARC is the centre for
what is officially designated 'Foreign Artefacts' – this means alien
artefacts. Crashed and recovered alien technology is stored there.
The DARC is where all the analysis of 'extraterrestrial biological
entities' – alien creatures – and back-engineering takes place.

Fouche says that the reason the US government cannot come
clean about what they are up to at Area 51 is because, since the
birth of the UFO phenomenon in 1947, it has consistently violated
people's constitutional rights. The government considers anything
that it cannot control a threat, he says. It cannot control the alien
agenda, so it tries to control any information surrounding it. People
who find out too much about UFOs or aliens either disappear or
have been killed, he says. The government would be held account-
able if the facts got out and it could not handle that.

David Adair

Another witness to what is going on at Area 51 is space scientist
David Adair. He became involved in the world of UFOs through

his lifelong passion for science and rocketry.

Adair was a child prodigy. He built his first rocket at the age of eleven. This was no fourth-of-July firework. He fashioned it from sophisticated alloys, using tools and fuels from his father's machine shop.

Then, in 1968, he set out to build a new type of rocket which used powerful electromagnetic fields to contain and harness the thermonuclear energy from a fusion reaction. Although this sounds exotic, it was not his original idea. He got the plans from the long-range planning division of NASA's Marshall Space Flight Center in Huntsville, Alabama. They had come up with the theoretical designs for fifty different types of engine. Only two of them used conventional liquid fuel or solid propellants, so fusion was the obvious the way to go. The one that Adair decided to build was a remarkable design. At the time he wondered why NASA had never made it themselves. Later he realised that they probably chose not to develop it for political reasons. If you developed an efficient fusion-based propulsion system, oil and gas would be redundant. Nevertheless the fourteen-year-old Adair saw the design's potential and, through Republican Congressman John Ashbrook, he got a $1-million grant to build it.

But the grant came with strings attached. The Department of Defense were involved. He was prohibited from telling anyone about what he was building. And for Adair the outside world ceased to exist as he worked on the rocket day and night for the next three years. In 1971, when Adair was seventeen, the rocket was ready to be tested. General Curtis LeMay, the project manager, decided that the rocket was too powerful to be tested outside a secure military facility, so he scheduled a test at White Sands Missile Range in New Mexico.

When Adair was at White Sands preparing for the test, a black DC-9 arrived. It was carrying Dr Arthur Rudolph, one of the designers of the Saturn-5 moon rocket. Originally Rudolph had worked on the Nazi German V-2 programme, but after the war he had been taken to America. Adair told Rudolph that, proportionately, his rocket was a thousand times more powerful than the

Saturn-5, and Rudolph was furious. When Adair was programming his rocket's guidance system, his military bosses gave him a precise location for the landing. The co-ordinates they gave him specified a place four hundred miles away in an area called Groom Lake in Nevada. This puzzled Adair as all the maps showed there was an empty dry lakebed.

After the rocket was launched successfully, Adair was told to get on board the DC-9. They flew him to Groom Lake and, as they came in to land, he could see the huge runways and a huge base that had not appeared on the map. This, he was informed, was Area 51.

When he arrived at Groom Lake, Adair thought he was there to collect his rocket. But he was bundled onto an electric golf cart and driven over to three large hangars. As he got close to the buildings, he could see that they were new, but they had been painted to look much older. The middle hangar was the area of two football fields. Once he was inside, warning lights began flashing, guard rails sprang up and an area of the floor about seven hundred square feet started to descend. Adair realised they were on a huge lift. It went down through solid rock and, when it stopped, Adair found himself the biggest underground space he had ever seen. It contained a lot of aircraft. Most of them were covered up, but he recognised one as the XB-70, an experimental aircraft. It was huge. But he also noticed a number of craft that were a strange teardrop shape with their surfaces perfectly smooth in all directions. The most peculiar thing about them was that they did not have any of the intake or exhaust ports that are needed by jet engines. In fact, they had no visible means of propulsion, yet they were surrounded by support equipment and looked quite capable of flying. Looking back, he now thinks that they used some kind of electromagnetic or flux-field propulsion.

Still in the golf cart, he was driven over to a big set of doors. The driver jumped out and put his hand on a panel. It flashed and the doors opened. We know these things now as optical hand-print scanners, but in 1971 they were the stuff of science fiction. Inside the air was cold and the lighting was strange. There was plenty of light, but nothing seemed to cast a shadow. He was then shown a huge engine that was about the size of a bus. It looked like two octopuses linked together by their tentacles. When Adair examined it, he realised it was some kind of giant version of the motor in his rocket.

His companions explained that this engine used a fusion reaction similar the one he had designed and they wanted his opinion on the firing mechanism. The whole situation struck Adair as bizarre. Why didn't they ask the people who built it, he enquired. He was told they were on leave. So Adair asked to look at their design notes. This seemed to annoy the people who had brought him there.

'Look son, do you want to help your country or not?' they said.

Adair believes that the engine was extraterrestrial in origin. Although it was huge, he could not see a single bolt, rivet or screw holding it together. The surface was perfectly smooth and, although the room was cold, it felt warm to the touch. Whenever he touched the surface, bluish white waves swirled out from his hands and disappeared into the material. They would stop each time he moved his hand away. He climbed up on top of the engine and looked inside. He saw a large container holding bundles of tubes. These were filled with some kind of liquid. Adair's overall impression was that it was organic – part mechanical, part biological. He realised it had been made using non-terrestrial techniques and materials.

He shrugged his shoulders and told his companions that he had no idea how the thing worked. The manufacturing techniques used were very different from anything he had ever seen before. He reasoned that it could not have been built by American engineers or by the Soviets. As it dawned on him that it must have been built using extraterrestrial technology, he got angry. Flying saucers had landed and the government were keeping it a secret. When Adair expressed his outrage at this, his companions shouted at him to get away from the device.

Adair does not think that the engine was working too well, though they have had three decades to work on it since then and he hopes they have been successful. He could certainly see the potential. Adair's own rocket was puny by comparison but it channelled enormous amounts of energy out of the back of the rocket for propulsion. He believes that the alien engine could have managed to contain all the incredible energy generated by the fusion reaction inside the propulsion system, producing a 'field effect' outside the craft. This would create a huge 'gravitation well' which would break through the fabric of space-time. Space would be folded back on itself, allowing the craft to travel vast distances in an instant, without exceeding the speed of light.

However, he is still angry that this device and other exotic craft are in government hands and all their amazing technology is hidden from the rest of the world. Meanwhile people at NASA are struggling to send small spacecraft to Mars. The fact that the US government are withholding knowledge of their contact with other civilisations he also finds incredible.

'These are ET civilisations we could learn so much from,' Adair says. 'When I think of all the ways that we could advance with this knowledge of ET contact, it makes me sick that this information is hidden.'

Since his visit to Area 51 in 1971, Adair has worked as a technology transfer consultant, redesigning space-programme technology for commercial applications. He has an office in Ventura, California. But he has not forgotten what he saw.

On 9 April 1997, Adair testified to a Congressional hearing in Washington, D.C. as part of the campaign for full UFO disclosure. The hearings were organised by the Center for the Study of Extraterrestrial Intelligence and gave key witnesses, including military personnel and pilots, the opportunity to lobby the US government. David Adair was under oath when he told the Congressional panel what he had seen in Area 51 and, unexpectedly, the Congressmen immediately got confirmation that he was telling the truth.

During his testimony, Adair mentioned that the device he had seen was covering in strange markings. He remembered what they looked like and drew them for the panel. Also giving testimony was an attorney from North Carolina named Steven Lovekin, who had top-secret clearance when he worked as a cryptologist at the Pentagon in the 1950s. As military aide, he had given regular briefings to President Eisenhower on UFO activity. In that capacity, he had been shown a piece of metal that he was told came from a downed flying saucer. It was covered in strange markings – the same markings Adair had seen in Area 51.

Wendelle Stevens

Wendelle Stevens' involvement with UFOs began in 1947 when he was assigned to the Air Technical Intelligence Center at Wright Field in Dayton, Ohio, home to the USAF's various in-house UFO study programmes, Sign, Grudge and Blue Book. That year, Stevens was sent from Ohio to Alaska to supervise a squadron of B-29 bombers that were being used to map the Arctic. However, he discovered there was a hidden agenda behind their polar mission. The B-29s were equipped with cutting-edge electronic detection technology and cameras to detect and film 'foo fighters', as UFOs were then known.

Stevens's security clearance was not high enough to allow him to see the footage the B-29s had shot before it was sent to Washington, but the pilots told him of their UFO encounters. Many of his pilots saw UFOs soar rapidly into the sky and fly off as the B-29s approached. In most cases, they caused electromagnetic disturbances to the plane's instrumentation, often affecting the engines. On one occasion a UFO approached a B-29 head on. Then, before they collided, it slammed into reverse, manoeuvred itself around next to the wing and stayed there.

Astounded by these revelations, Stevens asked his superiors if he could pursue an investigation into the UFO phenomenon. He was told he could do so only outside of official military channels. So, in 1963, after twenty-three years' active service, he retired and began a new career as a UFO researcher.

He began collecting newspaper clippings of UFOs from all over the world. Where photographs had been printed, he would write to the people who had taken them and ask for a copy. Now he boasts the world's largest collection of UFO photographs – over three thousand images in all – along with a vast library of UFO film and videos.

To establish the authenticity of the photographs, he visits the people who took them and investigates their encounter. He also examines their camera equipment and takes his own photographs from the same spot, so that he can compare relative scale and distances. After these preliminary checks, he subjects the photograph to a series of analytical procedures. Today he uses computer techniques. It was easier in the old days, he says, when all a photographic expert had to do was to make a large-scale blow-up and examine it with a magnifying glass.

Stevens is one of the few UFOlogists who had has made a career of studying contactees. In 1976 he was the first researcher to investigate the claims of Swiss contactee Eduard 'Billy' Meier, who was in telepathic contact with aliens and photographed their spaceships coming into land. At Stevens' behest, Meier submitted his evidence for analysis to scientists at McDonnell Douglas, IBM and NASA's Jet Propulsion Laboratory. Their results were inconclusive. However, computer analysis of one of Meier's pictures reveals a model next to a fake tree and models of flying saucers were found in Meier's home. Nonetheless, Stevens believes Meier is genuine.

Stevens decided to specialise in contactees because they presented a unique opportunity to learn about extraterrestrials and their possible agendas. If possible, he sets up a two-way dialogue, asking contactees to pose questions to the extraterrestrials for him next time they meet. Sometimes he gets an answer.

One of the most important contactee cases he investigated was that of Bill Herrmann, who lived in Charleston, South Carolina, near the Air Force base there. He and his wife repeatedly saw a UFO, which flew in a darting motion with sharp, angular turns, unlike the smooth turns of a plane. One night in 1977, when he was try to get a closer look at it through binoculars, Herrmann was abducted. He was enveloped in a beam of blue light, which drew him up inside the UFO. The extraterrestrials he encountered inside the craft were friendly. They came from one of the twin stars in the Reticulum system. When he asked them questions, he would hear their replies in English inside his head. They told him that the darting movements of their craft were made to avoid any radar lock-on. Radar-guided weapons had previously been responsible for the crashes of three of their ships. They also told Herrmann that they wanted their downed ships back and were prepared to negotiate, but the US government was too hostile to deal with. After this first abduction experience, Herrmann was invited back onto the craft another five times.

When Stevens began investigating the Herrmann case, he discovered that the Reticulans were sending Herrmann vast amounts of information when he was in a trance-like state. He transcribed the transmission in automatic writing. The result was numerous pages of text in a totally unknown alphabet, along with schematic diagrams of their propulsion system. The complex technical information he was provided with was way beyond current human scientific knowledge and Herrmann could never have acquired it from any terrestrial source.

From his work with contactees, Stevens has discovered that there are many different kinds of extraterrestrials. They come from different places and have different languages, morphologies, technologies and agendas. The largest group are the various humanoid species who often tell contactees that they come from the Pleiades star system. The next largest group are the well-known 'Greys', which again comprise a number of different races.

Stevens has also carried out research on Area 51 and tracked down Derek Hennesy, a former security guard who worked on level two of S4, the famous underground complex where Lazar had worked on alien propulsion systems. During his time there, Hennesy saw nine bays for flying saucer bays on level one. There were a further seven bays on level two with three identical alien craft in the first three bays. Hennesy also saw large tubes that contained the preserved bodies of dead Greys. After Stevens first interviewed Hennesy, Hennesy disappeared for a while. When he re-emerged he claimed to have no knowledge of what he had previously seen or said.

However, Stevens had another friend who works as an engineer at Area 51 and says it is engaged in bridging the gap between alien technology and our own. He has built simulators to train human pilots to fly flying saucers. There are two extraterrestrials at Area 51 who can fly alien craft. They have been trying to train humans to do this, but not very successfully. So far they are limited to flights within the atmosphere. They have not yet mastered flight in deep space, but they can hover using some kind of gravity propulsion.

Stevens thinks that there is little chance that the curtain of official secrecy surrounding UFOs will be lifted in the near future. The government have kept what they know a secret for fifty years and he expects them to do so for another fifty. Governments have far too much to lose from any official disclosure, he reckons. The impact on society would be incalculable. The only way the world's governments would admit to the reality of alien visitations is if a group of extraterrestrials makes its presence visible on a massive scale, he says. Stevens believes that there are signs that this may be about to occur in Mexico, where there was an explosion in the number of sightings in the 1990s.

Peter Gersten

For twenty years, New York criminal defence attorney Peter Gersten specialised in murder and drug cases. But then, in 1977, as the lawyer for the UFO group Ground Saucer Watch, he took the CIA to court and won. It was a historic victory for UFOlogy.

The suit was filed under the Freedom of Information Act. Ground Saucer Watch were trying to force the CIA to release just five UFO-related documents the agency had in its possession. But Gersten expanded the case. Under the FOIA it was as easy to create a lawsuit to get the CIA to release all the UFO document it had as it was to get just five. As a result, in 1979, the CIA was forced to release nine hundred pages of UFO-related documents – the first time that any US intelligence agency had ever released previously classified UFO information to the public. A further fifty-seven documents were withheld. But the case showed beyond any doubt that the CIA, which had previously denied any involvement in UFOs, had been studying them for years.

The documents not only confirmed the reality of UFOs and gave detailed descriptions of them, they also gave researchers access to numerous reports from credible witnesses – scientists, military personnel and law enforcement officers. Some of the documents released originated from other agencies. This confirmed that every other US agency had also been studying the UFO phenomenon and that the military had been involved in UFO research even before 1947.

Bolstered by this success, Gersten formed Citizens Against UFO Secrecy (CAUS), an organisation dedicated to breaking down the wall of secrecy surrounding the UFO phenomenon. Its aim is to force the government to come clean on what it knows about contact with extraterrestrial intelligence, and it believes that the public has the absolute and unconditional right to know.

In the early 1980s, Gersten continued his legal assault on the US intelligence community, taking the National Security Agency to court after the NSA refused an FOIA request for UFO-related documents that CAUS knew they had in their possession. In court, the judge asked the NSA's attorney how many documents had surfaced when they had processed the CAUS's FOIA request. He was told that it was classified information. Gersten told the judge that the CIA had told him that the NSA had at least eighteen documents. The judge then insisted that the NSA come up with a figure. The agency finally admitted that there were 135. But that was as far as it went. The NSA invoked the National Security Exemption, one of twelve exemption clauses built into the FOIA. To argue their exemption, the NSA used a twenty-one-page affidavit that was itself classified, and the case was dismissed.

Although Gersten was unsuccessful in obtaining the UFO documents, he did succeed in getting the NSA to admit that they held them. He took the appeal to the Supreme Court and, when it was dismissed, it made headline news. Even though he did not get the documents, he had succeeded in drawing great attention to the issue of UFO secrecy and highlighted the US Supreme Court's role in this cover-up. In further court actions, Gersten succeed in forcing the release of a heavily censored version of the NSA exemption affidavit and, in due course, most of the documents they withheld have been released.

Gersten is not optimistic about the efforts of various organisations – such as Dr Steven Greer's Center for the Study of Extraterrestrial Intelligence – to get the US Congress to hold open hearings on the subject of UFOs. He says that the idea of open hearings is inherently ridiculous because any discussion of UFOs involves a discussion of advanced technology. This is an area that the military keeps secret by invoking national security, while the corporations protect their developments by using patents. The elected officials of Congress are always up for re-election – every two years for Representatives and six years for Senators. They need money and are always vulnerable to the demands of special interests.

Getting Congress to grant immunity to people who may have to break secrecy oaths to testify would not help. Gersten points out the problems: 'Let's say you have a general who wants to testify in a Congressional hearing even though he is sworn to secrecy. He will naturally expect Congress to grant him immunity. However, the military will then question Congress's right to grant immunity and they would then have to fight it out in the courts, which could take years.'

Gersten finds it more effective to work through CAUS, which makes it possible for him to protect the privacy of any informant, through client–attorney privilege, but at the same time get the information out.

He used the Freedom of Information Act to try and pressurise the US Army into releasing documents relating to statements made by Colonel Philip J. Corso in his book, *The Day After Roswell*. Corso was willing to testify that he had seen the bodies of dead aliens in 1947 and that he had read alien autopsy reports in 1961. Gersten was ready to take the issue to court, so he filed an FOIA request with the US Army for the release of any documents they may have had supporting Corso's claims. The Army claimed it could find no documents and Gersten took them to court. But

Corso died and, on 26 April 1999, the case was dismissed. Gersten decided not to take that matter any further. Instead he filed a suit against the Department of Defense over Flying Triangles, in an attempt to find out what these mysterious craft actually are. While Gersten concedes that some of the sighting reports clearly describe advanced US experimental aircraft such as the TR-3B, which researcher Ed Fouche claims was built at Area 51, many of the reports could not possibly be the TR-3B. People have seen triangular craft that are half-a-mile wide. Some are seen at treetop level and over populated areas, shining beams of light on the ground. Witnesses also report seeing orb-shaped lights detach from these craft, fly around and re-attach. None of this can be explained in terms of advanced military technology.

Gersten sued the US government for damages after Betty Cash, Vickie Landrum and her grandson were abducted in Texas on the night of 29 December 1980. Gersten argued that as the UFO concerned was escorted by twenty Chinook helicopters it must have been part of a military operation. The case was dismissed on the grounds that the government denied all knowledge of the UFO and Gersten could not prove that it belonged to them.

Gersten is also bringing an unprecedented FOIA lawsuit against the CIA, the FBI and Department of Defense on the grounds that alien abduction can be viewed legally as a form of invasion. Article 4, section 4 of the US Constitution requires that the Federal Government protect the individual states against invasion, a provision that was enacted to persuade the original colonies to abandon their independent militias and join the Union. However, the Federal government are plainly failing in their duty to protect citizens of the States if those citizens are being abducted.

CAUS and Gersten have even more ambitious plans. As it is unlikely that the President is likely to open up all the files on UFOs in the foreseeable future, they want to find out for themselves. They are planning a privately funded mission to the Moon, to send back pictures from the Sinu Medi regions where some UFOlogists have locateed alien structures. Using existing technology, they estimate that their 'Project Destination Moon' would cost $12 million – small change to the likes of Bill Gates and Ted Turner.

'Think of all the money sponsors would make from the publicity if they funded the first civilian mission to the Moon, especially if alien artefacts were discovered,' says the ever-optimistic Gersten. 'The space programme is in the hands of the government and the military. We are all like virtual prisoners on this planet. This is a project that is just waiting to happen.'

Derrel Sims

Alien implant expert Derrel Sims is a former CIA operative and got involved in UFO research after being abducted himself. He has conscious recollections of multiple abductions between the ages of three and seventeen. He started researching in this field at the age of sixteen and has been at it for more than twenty-seven years. After leaving the world of covert intelligence, he rose to become chief of investigation for the Houston-based Fund for Interactive Research and Space Technology. There he concentrated on collecting physical evidence, as he believes that this is the best way to prove that UFOs and alien abductions actually exist.

He has investigated hundreds of cases of alien implants, some of which have been inside the body for up to forty-one years. Despite being foreign bodies, they trigger no inflammatory response. He says that the devices found are 'meteoric' in origin. Although some labs have said that this is impossible, 'double blind' tests had proved this to be the case.

Dr Roger Leir

For years, people doubted the reality of alien abductions. This was largely because abductees had no physical evidence to back their stories. One man changed all that – Dr Roger Leir. A podiatrist from south California, he was the first doctor surgically to remove an alien implant. Until his first operation in August 1995, they had been seen only on X-rays and CAT scans.

Leir had a long interest in UFOs and was a long-standing member of the Mutual UFO Network, where he gained an investigator's certificate. As an investigator, he attended a UFO conference in Los Angeles in June 1995, when he met Derrel Sims. Sims showed Leir a number of X-rays. One of them showed a foreign object in the big toe of an abductee. Leir was sceptical, but Derrel produced the abductee's medical records, which showed that she had never had surgery on her foot. Leir offered to remove it and this led to a series of operations on abductees.

He selects candidates for surgery by strict criteria, which were developed when Leir was working at the National Institute for Discovery Science. Anyone undergoing surgery had to be a suspected abductee – they had to have experienced missing time or, at the very least, seen a UFO. They had to fill out a form that determined how deeply they were involved in the abduction phenomenon. They also had to have an object in their body that showed up on an X-ray, CAT scan or MRI.

Some of Leir's patients would have a conscious memory of the object being implanted into their bodies during the abduction. But, more often, implants are discovered by accident. Some abductees find unusual lumps and scars that have suddenly appeared and go to their doctors to get them X-rayed. In one case, an implant was discovered during treatment following a car crash.

All Leir's patients are given a psychological examination before and after the implant is removed. Some of them experience a new-found sense of freedom after surgery. One abductee went straight back to her family, saying she wanted nothing more to do with UFOs.

Leir has, so far, operated on eight individuals and removed a total of nine objects. Seven of them seem to be of extraterrestrial origin. Five were coated in a dark grey shiny membrane that was impossible to cut through even with a brand new surgical blade. One was T-shaped. Another three were greyish-white balls that were attached to an abnormal area of the skin. Leir found that patients would react violently if the object was touched and often suffered pain in that area in the week before the implant was surgically removed.

During surgery, Leir discovered that there was no inflammatory response in the flesh around the implant. He found this surprising as any foreign object introduced into the body usually causes an inflammatory response. In this case, there was no rejection. He also found that the surrounding tissue also contained large numbers of 'proprioceptors'. These are specialised nerve cells usually found in sensitive areas, such the finger tips, which sense temperature, pressure and touch. There was no medical reason for them to be found where he found them, clustered around the implant. In two cases, Leir found 'scoop mark' lesions above the implants. In each case, Leir found that the tissue there suffered from a condition called 'solar elastosis'. This is caused by exposure to ultraviolet light, but it could not have been due to sunburn as only a tiny area was affected.

Leir found that the membrane surrounding the implants was composed of the protein coagulum, hemosiderin granules – an iron pigment – and keratin. All these three substances are found naturally in the body. However, a search of the medical literature revealed that they had never been found together in combination before.

The implants themselves would fluoresce under ultraviolet light – usually green, but sometimes other colours. In one case, Leir found that an abductee had a pink stain on the palm of her hand. It could be removed temporarily, but would seep back under the skin. Derrel Sims uses this fluorescent staining, which cannot be removed by washing, to detect implants. Leir believes that it is caused by a substance given off by the implant to prevent rejection.

A wide range of tests have been carried out on the implants Leir has removed. They are submitted to routine pathology tests to see if they are human in origin. When that draws a blank, they are sent for metallurgical testing and they have been examined under optical microscopes and electron microscopes, and analysed using X-ray diffraction techniques that tell which elements they are made of.

When the T-shaped implant that Leir had removed from one patient was magnified one thousand times under an electron microscope, a tiny fishhook could be seen on one end of the crossbar of the T, which Leir believes anchored the implant to the flesh. The other end was rounded off like the nose of a bullet, while in the middle there was a tiny hole into which the shaft of the T fitted perfectly. One of the rods had a carbon core, which made it electrically conductive. The other had an iron core, which was magnetic. An attractive force between them made them cling together. The shaft was encircled by a band of silicate crystals. Bob Beckworth, an electrical engineer who works with Leir, likened this to an old-fashioned crystal set, where a quartz crystal and a copper wire were used to pick up a radio signal.

Specimens were sent to some of the most prestigious laboratories in North America – Los Alamos National Laboratories, New Mexico Tech and Toronto University, among others. The samples were found to contain rare elements in the same isotopic ratios that are found in meteorites. When the labs were told that the specimens had been removed from body tissue, they did not believe it. For Leir, this is the smoking gun.

When you mine an element on Earth, the ratio of the various radioactive isotopes it contains always falls within a certain range. If you mine uranium, for example, it will always contain a certain ratio of uranium 234, 235 and 236. This will be roughly the same anywhere on Earth. But rock samples from the moon or meteorites contain completely different isotopic ratios. The isotopic ratios in the implants showed clearly that they were not of earthly origin.

Leir is not sure what the implants are for. They could be transponders or locating devices that enable alien abductors to track those they have abducted. They might be designed to modify behaviour – some abductees exhibit unexplained compulsive behaviour. They might detect chemical changes in the body, caused by pollution. Or they might be used to detect genetic changes in the body.

'If researchers such as Zachariah Sitchen are correct,' says Leir, 'and the human race is a genetically altered species, then it's possible that this genetic manipulation may still be going on and is something "they" wish to monitor closely.'

But what ever the implants are for, it is quite clear that they are extraterrestrial in origin. As Leir points out, if you find people who have been abducted by aliens and then find implants in them that have an isotopic ratio not found this planet, what other sane conclusion can you draw?

Tony Dodd

Ex-Sergeant Tony Dodd became interested in UFOs after having an encounter with one himself in 1978, when he was a police officer in North Yorkshire, England. He saw an object hovering about a hundred feet away. It had a domed top with four doors it. There were flashing lights around the sides, and three large spheres protruding from the underside. The whole structure was glowing bright white and it was silent. Dodd was sure this strange object was homing in on him, though it eventually floated off and landed nearby.

After he reported his sighting, his superiors told him not to talk to the press. This was standard procedure in the police.

Since then, he has seen seventy or eighty UFOs. Some of them are simply balls of light, anything from a couple of feet to thirty feet across. However, they seemed to contain some kind of mechanical device. He could often see a small, red pulse of light inside them, which created the aura of light. He has received hundreds of reports of these balls of light, which apparently fly in formation. That must mean they have intelligent controls, he reasons.

After retiring from the police force, Dodd took the opportunity to speak out. He devoted himself to UFO research full-time and became Director of Investigative Services for Quest International, one of the world's leading UFO societies, and he oversees the publication of their high influential *UFO Magazine*. For part of his time in the police, he was a detective and he uses police investigation techniques on UFO cases. His police background has taught him which lines of enquiry to pursue and how to encourage witnesses to come forward and talk. It has also given him contacts in intelligence and the military. This is not always an advantage. Dodd's mail is tampered with, even the registered packages that turn up. And the CIA have threatened to kill him, though he remains stoically unintimidated.

Dodd is the foremost expert on animal mutilations in the UK and believes the government know all about it. He also believes that elite forces in America and Britain had adopted a hostile attitude towards a certain type of alien because the aliens out there do not resemble us very closely. Aliens, he points out, do not necessarily have two legs and two arms. Indeed, in human eyes some are quite grotesque. This is the reason the aliens are abducting people and creating hybrids. The aliens, apparently feel the same way about us. When people are abducted, they are treated the way we treat animals on game reserves.

Abductions are never one-off incidents, he says. Dodd has never come across a victim who has been abducted in childhood and never abducted again. Once it has happened, it tends to occur throughout the victim's life. Dodd believes that abductees are being conditioned until they reach puberty. After that the visitors start taking sperm and eggs. Part of the alien's agenda, Dodd believes, is a genetic experiment to create human–alien hybrids. He has investigated cases where aliens have impregnated female abductees. The conception is not natural. It is performed with a needle that it inserted through the navel. Human babies can be conceived using similar methods, but our medical profession is years behind. Three months into the pregnancy, the abductee is picked up again and the foetus is taken from the womb. The resulting 'star children' have thin limbs, large heads and alien eyes and faces, though they have hair on their heads and small human noses.

One woman he knows has been impregnated twice and both times the aliens have taken the baby. When the woman was three months pregnant, she was out walking her dog and a strange light appeared in the sky. She knew they had come to take her baby. She also saw jars containing embryos, which were suspended in liquid, as if in an artificial womb. These jars were all around the walls of the room she was in.

In many of the cases that Dodd has investigated, the abductees seem to have a sixth sense. They get a feeling when they know the abduction is about to take place. However, people generally do not know that they have been abducted. The clue is when they know things that they would not normally know about.

He uses lie detectors in his investigations. But he also uses his knowledge of the subject and his police background to sniff out the hoaxers. He also uses hypnosis and always employs the same hypnotist. This is because the man does nothing more than put the subject under hypnosis. Dodd himself asks all the questions. This is vital because he does not want the witnesses to be led or have them given guides or pointers.

In abduction cases, Dodd also looks for physical evidence. Some abductees have strange marks on their bodies. In one case he investigated, a woman saw strange balls of light in the bedroom at night, and she had an inexplicable burn mark on her arm. The woman had contacted him after he had made radio broadcast about alien abductions and, although many of the things he had mentioned had happened to her, she wanted to be reassured that she had not been abducted.

He has also come across a case where an abductee set off a camera flash near an alien implant in his head. Something under his skin glowed green. It was about a quarter of an inch wide, but it did not seem to cause the man any pain.

On several occasions, Dodd has had a person under hypnosis who has ended up speaking as somebody else – one of the aliens, Dodd believes. When he asked them what right they had to abduct people, the alien voice replied: 'We have every right to do this, you do not understand the nature of things.' Dodd concluded that he was talking to a highly intelligent being.

Dodd has tried to develop this as a method of communication with the alien race and has come to believe that extra-terrestrial beings are involved in a collect-and-analyse experiment to study the human race. He is in regular communication with them, but they only divulge things piece by piece. When he gets impatient, they tell him that they have to take things slowly because the human race is not able to handle the truth. We have to be educated as if we were in infant school. Dodd finds this very spiritual.

This is why they are not communicating with all of us. We are not ready for the knowledge they possess. That is why Dodd himself is here. His role is to disseminate information, to learn from the aliens and to give what he knows out to humankind. His alien contacts have told him that he is some form of teacher. Apparently this was decided before he arrived on Earth as a child and it is why they are making contact with him. They have explained humankind's place in the universe and have told him that we are immortal spirits that go on and on.

'Every flower has its seed and every creature its destiny,' Dodd has been told. 'Weep not for those who have fulfilled their earthly obligation, but be happy that they have escaped that charge of material suffering. As the flower dies, the seed is born and so shall it be for all things.'

Dodd's contact with the aliens has religious aspects. He believes that they are a higher force and that they are responsible for us being here.

A.J. Gevaerd

A. J. Gevaerd is Brazil's leading UFOlogist, editor of the country's only UFO publication, *UFO*, and the director of the Brazilian Centre for Flying Saucer Research, the largest organisation of its kind in the country. He came to international attention in 1996, through his investigation of the famous Varginha case, where two extraterrestrials were captured after their spacecraft crashed in southern Brazil.

According to Gevaerd, there were numerous UFO sightings in the first few weeks of 1996. On the night of 19 January, two people reported seeing a spacecraft which had difficulty flying. At around 7:30 a.m. on the morning of 20 January, a number of people in the town of Varginha reported spotting a humanoid creature around. It had red eyes, a reddish-brown coloured skin and three small bumps on its head. Frightened residents called the Fire Department. They located the creature in an area called Jardim Andere and called the Brazilian army. By 10:30 a.m., army personnel and firemen had managed to net the creature and placed it in a crate. They then took it to the School of the Sergeant of Arms in the nearby town of Tres Coracoes.

Gevaerd discovered that a second extraterrestrial was found later that day. Three girls saw another creature cowering by a wall not far from where the first one had been captured. They told Gevaerd that it had a large head, brown skin, thick veins on its upper body and three protuberances on its head that looked like horns. At 8:30 p.m., a military vehicle with two policemen in it almost drove over a creature Gevaerd believes was the same as the one seen by the girls. One of the officers jumped out of the truck and grabbed it with his bare hands. He held it in his lap until they reached a nearby medical facility. Gevaerd discover that the creature was later transferred to the Humanitas Hospital in Varginha. The capture of the second creature occurred on a Saturday night when everyone was out on the streets. Many people saw the commotion and military trucks pulling up. In all, Gevaerd and his fellow researchers have interviewed over forty witnesses who saw the authorities capture the two creatures.

The aliens' UFO was first detected by an American satellite and the US informed the Brazilian military as part of an agreement between the two nations. So Brazilian radar was on full alert when the craft entered Brazilian airspace and it tracked the craft until it crashed into the state of Minas Gerais. Gevaerd has proof that both the US and the Brazilian government knew immediately that a UFO had crashed and knew roughly its location. Gevaerd tried to get details but there was a complete clamp down in the military. He believes that both extraterrestrials survived the crash, but died within a few hours of capture. The crash seems to have left them badly injured. The crash had occurred at around 3 a.m. When people saw them a few hours later, they were on their last legs.

'It could have been due to the crash,' says Gevaerd. 'Or perhaps the environment was not suitable.'

Gevaerd believes the US was involved from the start. He knows the creatures were later moved to the Hospital of Clinics at the University of Campinas. There were examined by a team of doctors, headed by Brazil's leading forensic scientist, Dr Furtunato Badan Palhares. In all, fifteen masked doctors examined the creatures' bodies, and seven of the team were non-Brazilians – probably US scientists. Gevaerd also thinks that the bodies were shipped to the US. A special US transport plane arrived on 26 January at Campinas, and he thinks that the bodies were taken to an Air Force base in North America.

'Everything indicates US involvement,' says Gevaerd. 'Our government does what it's told to do by the US. They co-operate with the US in return for favours.'

Since the Varginha incident, Gevaerd has consolidated his reputation by his investigation of 'Operation Saucer'. This began in 1977 when hundreds of UFO sightings came from an area along the Amazon river. Many people said they had been attacked by beams of light. Later many of them suffered symptoms of anaemia, although it is not clear whether this was due to loss of blood or to receiving a discharge from a UFO. The state authorities sent in teams of doctors, but they were attacked too. Eventually, the central government took the problem seriously, and, in September 1977, a team of twelve men from the Brazilian Air Force were sent to the area to investigate. They collected reports from over three thousand people who had seen UFOs and had been attacked by balls of light. This inquiry was called 'Operation Saucer' and was headed by Colonel Uyrange Hollanda, who told his story to Gevaerd in 1987, shortly before committing suicide.

The Operation Saucer team were ordered to talk to witnesses, document the evidence and get photographs – they took five hundred photographs of the UFOs in all. Hollanda's team were also ordered to see if they could make contact with the aliens and ask them why they had come. Although he got no direct answer to this question, Hollanda believed that the aliens were here to collect genetic material. Attacks usually took place when victims were alone and isolated. They would see a ball of light moving towards them. It would give them an electric shock, which would put them to sleep for several hours. When they regained consciousness, they would find small scars on their bodies, which Hollanda believed was caused by the extraction of tissue samples. But the damage was not just physical. Many victims suffered trauma and many were terrified. One fisherman who was attacked repeatedly was so terrified that he broke a leg while fleeing, Gevaerd says, but continued running despite his injury.

Hollanda reported seeing the craft associated with the attacks. They were sleek and teardrop-shaped with a large transparent area at the front, like a helicopter canopy, he told Gevaerd. On occasions, alien figures could be seen moving around inside. Towards the end of their investigations, short, humanoid, Grey aliens were regularly seen by the team. According to Gevaerd, the team's presence seemed to attract the interest of the extraterrestrials. Hollanda told Gevaerd that the aliens seemed to know everything the team did before they did it. For instance, if they decided to go up river, they would find the aliens waiting when they got there. Team members felt as though they were being observed. Eventually, the military team themselves fell victim to attacks. All members of the team were abducted. Hollanda himself was subjected to multiple abductions, during which he was examined both physically and psychologically by the aliens. He also told Gevaerd that he had acquired paranormal abilities as a result of his contacts.

However, these abductions caused Hollanda to lose his emotional stability. When Gevaerd interviewed him in July 1987, he broke down and wept. When he described his contact with the aliens he was obviously under great strain and was still plagued by strange phenomena years after he left the Amazon. He committed suicide two days before the first of a series of sessions of regressional hypnosis Gevaerd had arranged for him, thinking this might help.

Operation Saucer concluded that there was no doubt that the UFOs were responsible for the attacks. It also found that people were being abducted; some did not return. Gevaerd does not know why these abductions were happening, or why the aliens had such a special interest in the natives of the Amazon – although it is possible they conducted their experiments in this area because the people were isolated, living far from any protection.

Gevaerd finds the phenomenon of abduction a big puzzle. He has investigated cases where abductees have acquired paranormal abilities, including telepathic and healing powers, as a result. One case that Gevaerd investigated was that of Vera Lucia Guimaraes Borges, who was abducted in the 1960s when she was a teenager. She was living in the house of her grandmother in Valencia, near Rio de Janeiro, when she was woken one night by a noise and was lured into the kitchen. There she was confronted by a ball of light, which hovered in front of her. She promptly fainted. After this incident, Borges acquired remarkable paranormal powers, including the ability to diagnose a patient's illness by simply thinking about them. Under regressional hypnosis, she discovered that she had been abducted by two aliens – one male and one female in appearance – who had subjected her to a medical examination.

Doctors were called in by Gevaerd to test her diagnostic skills. She was 99 per cent accurate. One of the doctors was so impressed that he used her as a consultant. In one case, she told him that a young male patient had been bitten by a poisonous creature and told him which antidote to use.

'I know of many cases where abductees have acquired paranormal abilities,' says Gevaerd. 'Although abductions appear to have no obvious benefits, there are plenty of cases that illustrate we are visited by ETs who can help us do special things.'

However, Hollanda certainly did not benefit from his abduction, and other abductees gain nothing and end up traumatised. Although there are a lot of dedicated UFO researchers in Brazil, only a few are investigating abductions. As a result, Gevaerd is collaborating with the North American alien abduction experts Budd Hopkins and Dr John Mack, who he hopes will teach Brazilian investigators how to do abduction research.

'There is so much new data here that has not yet been seized upon by the media,' says Gevaerd. He believes that it could be the clue to an enigma: 'I'm convinced humanity, in a number of different forms, is spread out all over the universe. We are just a tiny fraction of what exists.'